When God Wrecks Your Romance takes away the fake shine of a *cool Jesus book* and replaces it with real heart and real faith. This book is about stumbling onto a new realization about the world, yourself, and God. It's about starting off as a starry-eyed Christian and becoming a mature and joyful lover of Christ. Amanda and Fr. Matt haven't written a vocations fairy tale, they've given us one better: a true-to-life example of what it means to "hear" God calling you forward and to choose your response. It's hard to think of a book this good at showing spiritual growth.

—*Steven Lewis*
Creator of Steve the Missionary

As a teen I always lay in bed asking God for this guy or that guy to be the one. And to be honest, I still do. This story gives me hope that God actually knows what He is doing. Jumping between perspectives, time, and even music lyrics, I feel like I know these two wonderful, funny, God-loving people. By their example, I hope to follow God's plan—even if right now it looks a little upside down.

—*Fabiola Garza*
Character artist at Disney Creative Group

Far from being a sappy romantic story with a predictable ending, *When God Wrecks Your Romance* is a beautiful and faith-filled account of love and the human desire for true happiness. At times thought provoking, at other times touching and tender, these reflections are honest and real.

—*Bishop William A. Wack, CSC,*
diocese of Pensacola-Tallahassee

When God Wrecks Your Romance is a well-crafted love story
that is relatable as well as endearing. From the opening line
I was hooked. Amanda and Matt portray a touch of
innocence that is captured by their use of creative prose and
individual perspectives along their cohesive journey.
Even as a non-practicing Catholic, this story had a way of
inviting me in and keeping me entertained.

—*Kim Collier*
Founder of Brown Girls Who Write

When God Wrecks Your Romance is just the book to remind
all of us that when God closes a door, He opens a window.
So often, we make plans and have dreams that we think are
exactly what we need. In reality, something even better is out
there waiting...if only we allow God to lead us.

—*Fr. Ronald Hutchinson*
Director of Priestly Vocations &
Director of Continuing Formation for Clergy,
diocese of Grand Rapids

Faith is confusing. Love is confusing. Does God have a
destiny for me or do I have free choice? Should I marry this
person or that person? As a fellow recording artist, I loved
exploring some of life's toughest questions through Amanda's
art and writing. This story is an honest, relatable, and fun
journey through youth, romance, family, music, and the
pursuit of God's purpose for our lives.

—*Nick De La Torre*
Singer, songwriter, producer

When God Wrecks Your Romance shows—through a genuine story that unfolds in the Catholic Church—that what matters to us in our heart of hearts also matters to God.

—*Esther Gomez Splawn*
Board member, New Wave Feminists

I wasn't quite prepared for what I would encounter reading a memoir about a couple who didn't end up together. To my great delight, this was a raw, honest, charming, and absolutely delightful read. *When God Wrecks Your Romance,* while gut-wrenching, heartfelt, and astonishing, is an effortless page-turner that will stir up emotions you didn't know you had and leave you feeling like you have new friends by the end.

—*Ryan O'Connell*
Filmmaker for Life Teen International

Both as the co-narrators and as characters in this story, we get a sympathetic and surprising sense of Amanda and Matt. We see them struggle courageously toward insight marked by actual faith: rugged, gritty, graceful, often marked by failure, but shaping us (as clay in the potter's hands) into the men and women we always hoped we would be.

—*Patrick Hannon, CSC*
English instructor and Pastoral Resident
at the University of Portland

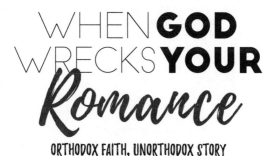

WHEN GOD WRECKS YOUR Romance

ORTHODOX FAITH, UNORTHODOX STORY

AMANDA VERNON & MATT FASE, CSC

PUBLISHED BY JOYFUL NOISE, INC.

2018

Photos by Deanna Rae Photography & Alessandro Photography
Cover design by Fabiola Tenorio
Typesetting by Russell Graphic Design

First Edition 2018
Printed in the United States of America
ISBN 978-1-7328050-0-2 [Paperback]
ISBN 978-1-7328050-1-9 [eBook]
Library of Congress Control Number: 2018958557

Published by Joyful Noise, Inc.
P.O. Box 1454
Chandler, AZ 85244
whengodwrecksyourromance.com

To All Saints Unplugged,
all the feels.

Contents

..

Chapter 10
THE ONLY ANSWER

Chapter 11
NEW BEGINNINGS

Chapter 12
SANTA CRUZ

EPILOGUE

P.S.

Introduction

In your hands is a coauthored memoir written by a newly ordained priest and a young married mother of four children. It's the story of two kids who fell for each other as teens, and, spoiler alert, ultimately did not end up together. It's pretty much the opposite of a quaint and dreamy Hollywood ending.

Yet it most certainly is a happily ever after.

We began writing this story at the request of a well-respected Catholic publishing company. However, after reading our book proposal, they didn't believe us. Yet those whose opinions matter most to us, namely, the Congregation of Holy Cross and Amanda's husband, knew it to be true. They encouraged us to continue writing this book anyway.

As coauthors, we offer two very different vantage points, so we take turns explaining our individual perspectives. Between chapters, you'll find original song lyrics highlighting the theme of each step in our journey. Because the narrative jumps between locations and years, we indicate the setting and time-frame with each new scene.

And now, to break down the words of our peculiar title: *When God Wrecks Your Romance: Orthodox Faith, Unorthodox Story.*

We speak of God from the perspective of the Roman Catholic Faith. Sometimes we use technical terms specific to Catholics (such as "sacraments" or "tabernacle"). We attempted to give some context for those terms without sacrificing our overarching narrative approach.

"Wrecks" is a bit tongue-in-cheek. We wanted the title to reflect our love of laughter, after all. In addition to its meaning of "demolish," there is also an Urban Dictionary definition of "wreck," which is "to enjoy completely and thoroughly." At the end of the story, you'll have to judge which one best fits this book.

In our mainstream society, the word "romance" carries quite a bit of baggage. (The term "romance novel," for instance, definitely evokes a different genre than this piece.) What we mean, rather, is "the excitement and mystery of love."

"Orthodoxy" denotes our commitment to the Catholic Church. We are faithful to her traditions and teachings, and to the authority of the pope and of the Magisterium. We hope the joy of our Catholic Faith is evident in the way we live our lives. We also pray that the beauty of the Church is reflected in the pages of this book.

In our Catholic community, our story is not rare. (Ask any priest, or any woman who has fallen for a guy who ends up joining the seminary.) Many ordained ministers have shared their accounts of being called into ministry. Myriad lay people have told the tales of their path to marriage. And yet, we have never seen a priest and a married person publicly disclose their shared journey in such detail as this. So although it is not unique, sharing our story together is unquestionably "unorthodox!"

Together, we invite you to reflect with us upon the words of Jesus Christ: *"Love one another as I have loved you."*

Thanks for listening,
Amanda Vernon
Matt Fase, CSC

In Real Life

Verse 1

More than my picture on a plastic screen
More than my name and my biography
More than my favorite football team
I want you to see the real me

Chorus

When we share a smile across the room
I wanna laugh and listen and love with you
Look at my eyes, here comes a surprise
I wanna be your friend in real life

Verse 2

More than, "It's all good. Fine. Like, whatever."
More than, "What's up? Tell me 'bout the weather."
More than indifferent, more than pristine
I want you to see the real me

Bridge

See my heart out on my sleeve?
Sometimes it breaks, sometimes it bleeds
But I'd rather let it break than tuck it away
I'm gonna let you see it, and I'm not afraid
Afraid, afraid...not afraid

PLANNED FAMINE
AMANDA

The Vernon House
Grand Rapids, Michigan
Sunday, March 15, 2009
8:50 A.M.

I can't believe we're about to have this conversation.

Sure, I always hoped this would happen, but I never dreamed it would be under these conditions. Although the time was getting late, I went slowly. Backing my bronze sedan down my parents' driveway was an acquired skill. *At least there's no snow on the ground.* After successfully steering out onto our sleepy, no-through street, I looked back at the little house.

Black shutters ornamented the windows around the red-brick exterior. White siding led to the peaked roof of the attic. *Our house feels so much more spacious inside than it looks from out here.* Apart from a brief stint away at college in Milwaukee, Wisconsin (and the first six months of my life, also in Wisconsin), I had lived on this city block of Grand Rapids, Michigan, all twenty-one years of my life. Grand Rapids was definitely my hometown, although my mom and dad kept their native-Wisconsin connection going strong.

There were two main rules in our family: you had to be Catholic, and you had to be a fan of the Green Bay Packers. Elements of those values could be observed even from the curb. An oversized green and gold flag flew prominently next to the front door, overtly displaying Packer pride (even though it was off-season). Set back a bit from the main entrance was the large window of our living room. Inside, a wooden cross, maybe four feet in height, hung on the back wall. Draped over its light-brown beams were white, satin letters proclaiming "P-E-A-C-E" to every passerby.

I shifted the car into drive and headed down to the main intersection. *Ah, the outskirts of the ghetto.* I grinned. My mother resented that particular description of our neighborhood. *Just teasing, Mom.* As the eldest of her children, I considered it a God-given responsibility to set a tone of playfulness around the house. Although a handful of our neighbors had lived on the street even longer than our family, many of these modest brick houses saw new residents every couple of years. A few childhood summers included incessant, blaring rap music from the live-in boyfriend of our neighbor across the street *(I hear you, Ghetto Man)*. In one house, college students rotated in and out between semesters at a local Christian college.

At the end of our street, like an anchor of stability on our urban block, stood a Christian Reformed church. Around the brick building was a large parking lot, great for learning to ride a bike. I turned right onto the main intersection. The roads were still quiet. Typically, I might be heading to Mass at this hour. But I had attended the night before, to make time for the upcoming conversation.

It's just breakfast. My heart was beating as if I were about to speak in front of a thousand people. *I've been waiting for this from the start.* A smile played around my lips. *I suppose I didn't know from the **very** start. The beginning was more like a joke. A happy, surprising, hopeful joke.*

A NEW SONG

Grand Haven, Michigan
February 23, 2002
Midmorning

Please let this be beautiful. Junior high students were still milling around the church auditorium as Deacon Ken gave an announcement that it was almost time for our opening prayer. I couldn't help smiling around Deacon Ken, my mentor and one of my favorite adults. *He thinks I'll do a good job leading music. That's why he asked me to be here.*

Deacon Ken was the youth minister of my home parish of St. Francis Xavier, a diverse, urban parish nestled in the heart of Grand Rapids. My family was highly involved in our church, to the point that St. Francis felt like my second home. Since I was homeschooled, theater and church were my primary social outlets. And so, Deacon Ken's invitation to lead music for this regional junior high youth retreat was an exciting honor.

I hope they sing with me! Arranging the chord charts on the music stand of the digital keyboard, I sensed several of the retreatants studying me. It wasn't a rare occurrence. Receiving lingering looks was pretty routine, on stage or off.

My mom told me that people used to stop her in the grocery store to comment on my appearance as a baby. I had golden-brown skin and bright blue eyes back then, an ambiguous-looking blend of my father's African American heritage and my mom's Swedish and Italian ancestors. By the time the awkward preteen phase passed (*hello and goodbye, acne!*), my eyes settled into their green hue. Braces had straightened the adult teeth that had grown in crookedly, and the attention resumed.

Taking a deep breath, I prayed in my heart. *Shine through me, Jesus. Help them see something of You when they look at me. Help them hear Your voice when they hear mine.*

"*Check one, check two.*" Everyone looked up expectantly.

"Welcome to the Planned Famine retreat," I said. Mostly blank stares looked back at me from the eighty or so students gathered.

At Deacon Ken's request, the parish of St. Patrick in Grand Haven, Michigan, had agreed to host sixth-, seventh-, and eighth-grade students from their own community, together with students from a smattering of other local churches. I was considered a teen leader, since I was a high-school freshman. Even so, with my fourteenth birthday at the start of the school year, I was young for my grade. *Some of these eighth graders are older than I am.*

I continued speaking in the microphone, explaining the meaning behind the title of our retreat. "We're really glad you came this weekend! During the next couple of days, we won't be eating much food, as you know. That'll help us to remember to pray for people who go hungry on a daily basis."

They all continued to watch me. Their nonverbal feedback wasn't particularly encouraging, collectively. I smiled bigger, nonetheless, and continued. "One of the ways we'll be able to pray this weekend is by serving in the local community. Another way, which is probably my favorite, is by singing together." *Maybe they're just nervous about doing something new.*

"Would you all please stand for a couple opening songs?" *If they can see my excitement, maybe they'll catch on.* "Let's make this a prayer! If you're comfortable with it, you could open up your hands to the sky as a sign of your openness to God's love."

Sharing music so others could enter into prayer was exhilarating. Gratitude welled within me, even as the students shyly followed along. *I trust You to do something beautiful in their hearts, Lord.*

MEETING MATT

February 23, 2002
Late morning

Deacon Ken cleared his voice into the mic, and then said, "We just spent time connecting with God through praise and worship, and we heard John's amazing story of escaping poverty in Sudan. We're now about to head to a homeless shelter to share the love of Christ with those who face poverty right here in West Michigan! First, you may get up to stretch your legs. Since many of you come from different churches, try to make at least one new friend before our next activity."

I clicked the power switch off and folded up the binder of chord charts. *Well, the keyboard's kind of clunky, and my voice felt a little nervous. I tried my best, though.* Aside from several rambunctious boys playing hacky sack, kids were huddled in tight clusters around the auditorium. *Maybe I could help them meet each other.* Toward the back of the room, a few students I hadn't seen before were laughing and talking.

Approaching their group, I heard a girl with glasses and brown hair asking, "You do improv? What is that?"

The boy who answered was thin, not quite as tall as I was, and he wore a bright red visor around his light-brown hair. "It's where you improvise a story or a skit on the spot. You have to be able to think on your feet. Which is tricky, since normally, thinking happens in your brain."

"Hey, how's it going?" I asked as the group turned toward me. "Which church are you guys from?"

The boy's fair skin became flushed. His gray eyes widened, and the tips of his ears turned red at the simple question. When no other words emerged from his previously animated face, the girls chimed in.

"We're from Our Lady of Consolation Parish in Rockford! What about you?"

"St. Francis Xavier in Grand Rapids," I explained. The girls and I exchanged small talk about our ages, where we went to school, and what we liked to do for fun. "I'm Amanda, by the way," I added. Looking toward the boy, I said, "So, it looks like your visor's meant for me!"

He only glanced searchingly among the other girls. *Am I embarrassing him? I thought he'd want to play along.* "Your visor has an 'A' stamped on the front. My name is Amanda." Just then, two students from the St. Francis youth group ran up to us.

"Hey, Krista. Hi, Mary." I smiled at the popular eighth graders. We had grown up singing together in the children's choir, which my dad directed.

With a mischievous grin, Mary turned to the boy. "What's your name? Nice visor!"

"I'm Matt," he replied in a high, slightly scratchy voice. Mary promptly snatched the visor and threw it to Krista. *Now it looks like we're fighting for his attention. That's not what I had in mind.* I was happy to see members of different youth groups interacting with each other, though. It seemed like the right time to apply the number-one rule of show business: *Always leave 'em wanting more.*

"See you guys later," I called out over their giggles.

As Krista tossed the visor back to Mary, Matt snatched it out of the air. Before I could make my exit, his outstretched hand extended the visor in my direction. *Well, this is unexpected.* The apprehensive but hopeful glint in Matt's eyes made me laugh. Setting the visor on top of my dark brown curls, I walked away without a backward glance.

RETHINKING THINGS

February 23, 2002
After dark

Unrolling my shiny purple sleeping bag the night of the Planned Famine, my stomach growled.

Some people feel this hungry every night, I reminded myself. Even on an empty stomach, it had been a very full day. Reflecting on the retreat, an entirely new paradigm came into view.

Serving at the homeless shelter had been fun and hands-on. Some of us cleaned the dining room chairs. Others sorted clothes or canned goods. During downtime, I helped organize improv games I'd learned in theater camp over the summer. Matt rose to the challenge and had us all rolling with laughter. *That must be why my sides are sore.*

That evening, instead of eating dinner, we held Eucharistic adoration. In a prayer unique to Catholics, we reverenced the Body of Christ under the appearance of bread. *It's one thing to believe Jesus is there, but hidden. It's so amazing to see signs of Him, though.* Beyond the candles and the soft singing, the peacefulness on everyone's face and the sincerity of their prayers were palpable.

Following adoration, all the kids on retreat had gone late-night bowling. Matt and I played as a team against Kevin and Ida (better known as "Chiquita"). Petite and vulnerable on the one hand, Chiquita's spunk, on the other hand, never ceased to entertain. *Kids who ignore her because of her cerebral palsy don't know what they're missing.* As her "Angelita," I always looked out for her with a fierce, sisterly protection.

Matt seemed psyched to be with my friends and me. His smile was way excited since I started wearing his red visor. His innocent exuberance caused me to reconsider a problem that had been troubling me for the past several months.

Fluffing my pillow in the darkened schoolroom, I sat cross-legged on my sleeping bag. *From the outside, I probably look really happy. And I used to be. On the inside, though…*

I was disappointed in what I had learned about boys … *it's such a letdown.*

A few older boys at theater camp the previous summer had paid me particular attention. At first, their flirtation seemed flattering. But when one of the boy's teasing turned to nonconsensual caresses, I felt frozen. *Was that my fault? Was I asking for it because I liked the attention?* After several similar incidents, I had asked the same questions of an upperclassman. Her guidance came as a jarring reality check.

"He doesn't really like you. He just wants to see how far you'll let him go," she stated candidly. The response felt like a blow to the gut. But it was her final bit of advice that sunk like a dagger into my thirteen-year-old heart. Apathetically, she added, "That's just the way guys are."

I had replayed her words again and again that summer. I measured them against the experiences with the boys from theater camp. Against the not-so-subtle objectification of women on the radio and television, and even against conversations caught from adults. "Men put up with a lot from women, because of sex," I had heard.

She was right. Guys only care about my body.

The conclusion reshaped my heart in an instant. Dreams of having a husband and a family of my own someday suddenly seemed pointless. *Who wants to get married if it's an agreement to be used for the rest of your life?* My self-image began plummeting. I had long hoped that my appearance would lift others' spirits and point them to God, the source of beauty.

That's not the way this works, I guess.

Someone nearby was shifting in her sleeping bag, and whispers arose from Mary and Krista in the far corner. I reviewed a mental list of guys who had made sexual advances toward me that year. *Grown men at the YMCA, older boys at theater camp, guys who chat with me online . . . .* The list was daunting. Their jeering looks and abrasive comments confirmed my fears.

And then there was Matt.

If guys only care about my body, why does he seem so excited to be around me? Matt's stunned expression from our first conversation came to mind. *It's pretty obvious that he thinks I'm cute.* But there was something more.

The way Matt tried to make me laugh, how he listened when I talked, and just the light in his eyes when he looked in my direction . . . . *It's like he really sees me. Who I am, on the inside.* I recalculated our age difference as I slid into my makeshift bed. *Clearly, I'm not interested in him romantically, though. I look at least three years older than him.*

All was quiet now, except for Mary and Krista, who were giggling in hushed tones.

On the other hand, Matt said his fifteenth birthday is coming up this summer. He'll probably get taller soon. With a conflicted sigh, my heavy eyelids rested. Then a most wonderful idea welled up in my heart.

What if I'm wrong? My eyes popped back open. *What if what I've been thinking about boys isn't true?* The prospect of being wrong had never felt so hopeful. *If Matt likes me just for being myself, maybe that means some guys really care about girls for more than just our bodies. And maybe one of them could really care about me someday.*

The darkened room had fallen silent. And I fell asleep.

PLANNED FAMINE
MATT

Anna's House
Grand Rapids, Michigan
Sunday, March 15, 2009
8:50 A.M.

I made the sign of the cross as I slid into the booth of the breakfast cafe. *In the name of the Father, and of the Son, and of the Holy Spirit.* I hadn't even placed an order yet, but the simple gesture—swiftly crossing my right hand from my forehead, down to my chest, and then over to each shoulder—always brought me a sense of peace.

Thank you, Lord, for the gift of life today, for the chance to be, and to do your will. I trust that you are here with me in this moment. Come, Holy Spirit, open my heart to your guidance. Amen.

Anna's House was the name of this simple breakfast and lunch restaurant on the north edge of Grand Rapids. That was the side closest to my parents' place in our suburban hometown of Rockford.

I had a wonderful childhood filled with family, laughter, campfires, and faith. Our home was a bit cramped for our family of seven, but that just meant it was better to be outside. Halfway down a secluded private drive, it was perched on a hill that overlooked a sprawling yard, wild fields, and the forest. Growing up, my family drove north into the woods far more than south into the city. That was still my preference.

The sleepy little spot, Anna's House, barely felt like it was in the city at all, though, especially on Sunday morning. *Why am I so nervous? It's just breakfast.*

I was raised to know food was of ultimate importance. *And it still is, even now that I'm twenty-one.* Mealtime was always a central part of life as a kid. When my dad called home from the office letting us know he was on his way home, things would kick into high gear. Mom, who had already been busy cooking, would shout out our names as she drafted each of us five kids into service, setting the table or stirring the pot. When everything was finally in place (with at least one of us needing a threat from the wooden spoon), we would begin the meal with a simple prayer over the food.

"Still waiting on someone?" Turning from the window, I saw a waitress standing by the table, a warm smile on her face. Hash browns, eggs of every style, stacks of pancakes, and piles of glorious bacon passed by on servers' arms.

"Uh, yes, yes I am." *She'll be here, right? She was the one who wanted to meet, after all.*

"Would you like something in the meantime?"

"Coffee would be great."

I wouldn't have been this excited for coffee the first time we met. That had been years before I developed an appreciation for that delightful wake-up fuel. There was a lot I didn't fully appreciate then. But heck, back then I was only fourteen. *She's really coming, right?*

A NEW SONG

Grand Haven, Michigan
February 23, 2002
Midmorning

There are so many people here I don't know. It's true there were some familiar faces. In light of my eighth-grade graduation in a few months, I had looked forward to this event as the final retreat with my middle school youth group. Far fewer of them came than I was hoping.

"Youth group" was the general term assigned to those middle-school and high-school teens who gathered weekly at my local Catholic church, Our Lady of Consolation, or OLC. The purpose of our meetings was to deepen our faith, but it was just as much a social time as it was religious education. There were games and songs and all manner of snacks. Sometimes it felt foolish, but other times, when I stopped worrying about being cool, I could sense that it was opening me to something more.

Although I did enjoy the new friends I was making, the main reason I went was because my parents wanted me to. Faith was important to my family, so I went to the youth group—on the weekends we weren't up north, that is.

"Up north" is the term used by Michiganders to describe any outdoor recreation that occurred away from their home. As you travel north in Michigan, the natural beauty increases as the population decreases. Just about everyone I knew had a little weekend spot, a cottage on a lake, or a cabin in the woods. I spent countless weekends with my family, camping in one rustic campground or another. My dad, my older brother, and I made good headway working through the book *Canoeing Michigan Rivers: A Comprehensive Guide to 45 Rivers.*

But I couldn't always be up north, and I enjoyed youth group well enough. *There are a few other youth groups here. I don't recognize any of them. I'd definitely prefer to be out in the woods.*

One of the other groups, the one from St. Francis, was much more diverse than mine. Granted, since the OLC youth group was made up exclusively of white, middle-class suburban kids, any diversity would be more diverse. Over the speakers, a tall, gray-haired man said, "Hey, everyone! I'm Deacon Ken Baldwin. We're about to get started. Amanda's just about ready to lead us in song, so find a spot!"

I looked for a place to drop my sleeping bag and my backpack, which had almost nothing in it. One end of the room had a large white projection screen and a big keyboard. There was a young woman setting it up. She obviously knew what she was doing as she adjusted the settings and plugged in the various electrical cords. *Wow, she's pretty! I can't believe they got a high schooler to lead music for us. Usually it's a music director from one of the parishes. I bet she's not older than seventeen.*

I found the rest of the kids from my group and set my bags down by theirs. "Where are we supposed to sit?" I asked. "I guess just anywhere," came the reply from Jake. I didn't really get to know Jake until this year at youth group, besides never talking to him in the one class we had together the previous year. I suppose that was one of the reasons for coming on retreat, to get to know the people in my youth group better. I told myself it would be fun to meet some kids from the other groups too.

Meeting other people was only part of the reason I now stood awkwardly on the edge of a room filled mostly with strangers, some seemingly stranger than others. *This will be a good opportunity to grow in my faith. I'm getting older, my faith needs to grow up too.* The "famine" part of this "Planned Famine" was pretty intriguing. Going without food would be a new experience for me. *If Jesus fasted for forty days straight, I can do it for two.* Well, an evening and a morning, anyway.

While the lack of sustenance wasn't particularly exciting, the community outreach aspect was even more unknown. The idea of going downtown, on purpose, to work with the economically disadvantaged was even further outside my experience than being hungry. *But Jesus loved the poor and the lonely. I need to, too.*

"Check one, check two."

Even her voice is pretty. The young woman, who must've been the Amanda who Deacon Ken mentioned, was having more success than the deacon at gathering the attention of this nervous and excited group of kids. Long, curly hair framed her mocha complexion. *How could she **not** hold your attention?*

She stood behind the keyboard with the easy confidence of having done this countless times. The sly smile on her lips reinforced the confident stance and added a layer of mystery and sass. *Even after the two plays I've been in, I've never been that comfortable on stage. Besides, acting is about pretending to be someone else. Up there with only a keyboard, she's just herself.*

Amanda's smile broadened as she surveyed us kids. Proceeding to offer some background on the theme of the retreat, she encouraged us to pray along with her. *With our voices, and even our hands?*

She gave the invitation with such enthusiasm that I found myself taking a step closer. I was not a good singer, but I did like to sing, as long as no one was listening. I was not nearly as excited as she was to do anything that was going to draw extra attention to myself, especially if I wasn't good at it. *I am open to God's love, though.*

As the music started, I raised my hands up to about my waist.

The song was one I knew. Still, I didn't want to sing loudly. For the second time in as many minutes, Amanda pulled me out from focusing on myself. This time it wasn't just her voice, it was also the way she played. The notes were fast, fierce, and precise. Three semesters of marching band still left me plunking out notes. I had learned you could be accurate, or you could play fast. Yet there she was, playing fast and flawlessly. *And she's singing so boldly. She's letting us see a real part of her heart, and she isn't even afraid we'll make fun of her for it!*

Amanda prompted us to sing along. *There are too many people around. What will they think of me?* A few more joined in and some even raised their hands up high. She continued to sing out, a beautiful prayer to Jesus.

This girl is someone I would sing for. So I did. *Her voice is loud enough to cover mine, anyways.*

Through opening up to the music and the lyrics, my nerves dissipated. Amanda had said these were prayers, so I sang them right to God. As the song ended with her working the keys in gentle strokes, I felt hopeful about coming to know Him better that weekend.

MEETING AMANDA

February 23, 2002
Late morning

After the music stopped, we listened to the personal testimony of someone who grew up in war-stricken Sudan. When everybody started to break back off into groups again, a crushing self-consciousness replaced the moment of selfless connection to God. *Other people were praying and singing too. No one is going to make fun of me for it. I hope.*

Following Deacon Ken's instructions, I went to get a drink. I passed some girls talking in serious and hushed tones. A group of guys had started playing hacky sack. I was pretty good myself. *Maybe I could join them.*

Some of the girls from my group were talking in a close clump. Thankfully, they didn't scoff as I walked up, and instead, they brought up seeing me in the school play the year before. I mentioned being in theater class, including my favorite activity: improv comedy.

"You do improv? What is that?" asked Sarah.

"It's where you improvise a story or a skit on the spot. You have to be able to think on your feet. Which is tricky, since normally, thinking happens in your brain." *That got a good laugh. Keep it rolling. They all seem to be happy talking to me. They must have been singing along too.*

Coming from a big family had a number of perks. Always having relatives and siblings of all ages around meant that I was used to talking with girls. *Just like cousins, right?* It was more difficult when I had a crush, though. The few dating relationships I had already ventured into were short-lived and light.

Talking with girls is way easier in a group of friends, like this. Plus, we're only in middle school, after all. I don't need to feel uncomfortable. We are all on the same level, right?

Before the next joke made it out, I saw Amanda walking toward us. *Wow. I cannot believe she got me to sing that much. She is beautiful, and talented, and open—and she's walking right up to me. Crap crap crap!*

Thoughts about what I should do and say raced through my mind as she struck up a conversation. I did catch that she had turned fourteen last September. *Wait . . . she's . . . three months younger than me!?* And the mention of her grade. *Already a freshman. Maybe that's why she seems so mature.*

"I'm Amanda, by the way. So, it looks like your visor's meant for me!"

Oh, my gosh, she's smiling at me! Why? Everyone's looking at my visor. Stupid thing, why did I even wear it?!

"Your visor has an 'A' stamped on the front. My name is Amanda." *Ohhhh, I see. Cool, very cool.*

Just then, two other girls ran up. Clearly they knew Amanda.

"Hey, 'Manda! Whatcha doin'?" one girl interrupted loudly.

"Hey, Krista. Hi, Mary," Amanda said.

Quick as a wink, Mary spun toward me. "What's your name? Nice visor!"

"I'm Matt," I said as calmly and coolly as I could. Unfortunately, my traitorous voice undermined my efforts and broke in the middle of my name. Mary snatched the visor from my head and threw it to Krista. The girls seemed to be enjoying this game of keep away far more than I was.

"Well, I'm gonna get ready to head to the shelter. Nice talking with you, ladies. See ya, Matt," said Amanda.

She must think we're so childish.

Krista gave the visor a low arcing toss back to Mary. *Perfect.* I grabbed it out of the air. *Gotcha.*

Well, the only one who seemed to appreciate this was Amanda, and it does have an 'A' on it. Before she could walk away, I extended the visor to her. Our eyes met. *I should not have done this. She thinks I'm stupid. What do I do now?*

Amazingly, she laughed. A bright, crisp laugh brimming with joy. *I want to make her laugh again.* She took it with a cool smile and slowly put it on, working her long, dark hair around it. Swiveling on her heel, she swiftly stepped away, taking my visor and my instantaneous affection with her.

A NEW UNDERSTANDING OF AN OLD FRIEND

"In a few moments, we'll have some time of Eucharistic adoration," Deacon Ken told us. "In the Gospel of John, chapter six, verse thirty-five, Jesus says, 'I am the bread of life.' And when Jesus shared the Last Supper with his friends the night before he died, he said, 'This is my body, which will be given for you; do this in memory of me.'"

There was an excitement in his voice as Deacon Ken explained that we were about to be part of a miracle, that we were about to experience God in a new way. A host, a simple piece of bread, became the Body, Blood, Soul, and Divinity of Jesus Christ through the power and promise of God at Mass.

He continued speaking while someone dimmed the lights. Only candles illuminated our faces as we listened. "At Mass we follow Christ's command to remember him. We receive Communion, and are fed with this presence of Christ.

"Tonight," he told us, "we are given the opportunity to marvel at, seek after, and listen to our God who is present here among us."

And with that, the music started. The tone was serious and slow as the monstrance was brought in. I could see what looked like a small white piece of unleavened bread in the middle of the shining, gold monstrance. I knew that even here, before a group of teens in widely varying stages of engagement, God was trying to reach us.

"Jesus," Amanda sang out. She was calling out to Him, naming the one who was present in our midst.

"Jesus," she continued softly singing, tenderly calling out to a friend.

"Jesus." I meekly added my voice to the song.

"Jesus." I called upon Him whom I had heard about all my life.

"Jesus," whom I knew and believed was my savior, the Son of God and my Lord.

"Jesus." The music crescendoed, raising my prayer with it. The notes swelled as I continued to sing out the name of Jesus. And then there was silence. I found myself staring into the monstrance, at the host in the center. I believed that Jesus was present in the Eucharist, but there was more. The music, the talks, and the prayers of that retreat had built upon what I already had been taught and opened up my heart. In that new openness, I found Jesus, present within myself. He was not merely a Bible character from long ago. I met Him as a friend, so very close to me.

SAVORING THE MOMENT

Unrolling my favorite sleeping bag that night, my stomach grumbled. I had gotten a new perspective on so many things. Between serving at the homeless shelter, playing improv games, having Eucharistic adoration, and even going bowling, the day had been surprisingly awesome. Hanging out with Amanda all night, her bright smile shining out from under my red visor, was far more than I had hoped for or expected from the day.

Looking down at my sleeping bag, I realized that I didn't bring a pillow. *Well, I've spent plenty of nights in this sleeping bag on more uncomfortable and colder surfaces.* I balled up my sweatshirt as a substitute pillow. Most of the other guys were still meandering into the room. We had at least fifteen minutes before lights out.

Man, I'm tired. Between working at the shelter and staying up late at the bowling alley, everybody must be wiped. "Thank you, Lord," I prayed in a whisper. *Today was a good day. And You were with me through it all. And tomorrow will be even better! Especially with Amanda leading the songs.* She was talented, kind, and had so much faith…. She was beautiful inside and out.

One last thought for the day drifted groggily across my mind. *Are the lights still on?*

With This Ring

Verse 1

On my hand I wear a sign
Of a solemn vow of mine
The hope of living chastity
A life that glows with purity

Chorus

And with this ring
I promise
To save my heart
My mind, my body
For the one who means
Much more to me
Than anything
This world can offer
With this ring
I'm waiting for the one
Whom God has saved for me

Verse 2

When temptation seizes me
I have this ring reminding me
That my Father's on my side
Gracing me
My joy, my guide

RED VISOR
AMANDA

Grand Rapids, Southeast side
Sunday, March 15, 2009
8:58 A.M.

Looking down from the red light, I scooped up my cell phone. *Time for voice-to-text.*

"Hey Matt, period. I am on my way, period."

Send.

What's with the butterflies? Take a deep breath, Amanda. It's not going to be like seeing each other the summer when we were fourteen. The light changed. I turned onto the open expressway. Rather than calming down, my heart rate increased as the car accelerated. A few definitive touchpoints at fourteen absolutely set a course for the rest of my life.

Zooming along the highway, I saw my phone light up with Matt's text: "Okay, see you soon." I shook my head at how much could change in an instant.

A PROMISE RING

The Vernon House
May 18, 2002
After dark

A few months after the Planned Famine retreat, preparations were under way for my confirmation. Preparations, such as my daylong confirmation retreat, which had just concluded. And preparations like extra chores.

*Why do you have to work **more** when you're from a big family? You're the eldest of seven kids. You're having a confirmation party tomorrow! But first, you win the prize of washing the floor!* That particular night, cleaning proved to be a constructive outlet for my adolescent angst.

I was going to receive the sacrament of Confirmation the next day, in a group of about fifty other eighth- and ninth-grade students from St. Francis Xavier Church. I wasn't upset about the upcoming ritual. That part was exciting.

My parents baptized me as an infant, which of course I couldn't remember. At baptism, a priest or deacon welcomes a new member of the Church by pouring water over the baby's head and saying the words, "I baptize you in the name of the Father, and of the Son, and of the Holy Spirit." At confirmation, the bishop would mark our foreheads with oil in the shape of a cross, praying for the Holy Spirit to descend upon us and enkindle the spiritual gifts received through baptism.

I felt ready to be confirmed. Over the course of the school year, my parents had sent me to "confirmation class." It was an educational course at church, held every other week. Whereas youth group was great for building a group of close friends of the same faith, confirmation class was more formal, instructional, and focused on the history of our faith tradition. And that was all in addition to the instruction at home.

In the months leading up to confirmation, my parents encouraged a greater awareness of God's guidance in the daily happenings of my life—particularly in any future dating relationships. One of my favorite Bible verses from childhood stood out as a crystallization of what they were trying to teach me: *"For I know the plans I have for you, says the Lord. They are plans for good and not for evil, to give you a future and a hope."* Confirmation seemed like a significant moment to claim that promise for myself.

No, it wasn't my confirmation that was upsetting. It was my "Confirmation Crush."

David Shaheen. Olive skin. High cheekbones. Raven black hair. He was, by far, the most attractive boy in confirmation class. Forcefully dunking a rag into a bucket of sudsy water, I replayed what happened with David earlier that day.

In the very first session of our confirmation retreat, I had admitted my crush to a new friend who had joined our parish that year. Ironically, my new friend promptly introduced herself to David and decided to spend the rest of the day with him. To my dismay, that evening, she pulled me aside to say, "I have a crush on David too! I'm *so* sorry. Could you take a picture of the two of us together?"

Their dating relationship appeared imminent. Recalling their overt flirting made my stomach hurt.

Some friend. I shook my head and pressed harder against the wood-laminate flooring. *What do I care if another girl dates David Shaheen?*

In the midst of my floor washing and fuming, my dad called out, "Amanda, come on over here. We have something to give you." *Is it a mop? 'Cause that could be helpful.*

"Coming, Dad!" I replied, forcing a pleasant tone. *Don't mind the rolled-up sleeves and pant legs. They come with the job. Feel free to call me Cinderella.*

My dad was seated on the couch next to my mom. My god-mother was there too, perched on the edge of an armchair with her camera in hand.

"These are for you." My dad handed me a white envelope with "Amanda" scrolled across the front, plus a little black leather box.

Taking the gifts, I looked up at my mom inquisitively. She gave me a gentle grin and a nod of affirmation. I dropped to my knees on the floor, and then sat back against my heels. Sliding my fingers along the back of the envelope, lined paper peaked out from inside. Unfolding the letter, the paper revealed my dad's handwriting.

A Promise Ring

Dear Amanda,
I pray that this ring will be a symbol of your purity and chastity, which are gifts from God.

By accepting this ring, you are making a promise to me to remain a virgin until the evening you receive the sacrament of Holy Matrimony. Just as God has given you free will to choose chastity or a life of sin, so do I give you this ring.

Please wear this ring as a reminder of your promise to me. If you someday choose to break your promise, know that I will love you no less. Most promises are made at a time when breaking a promise is unfathomable.

My face streamed with tears. The sound of Mom and Dad sniffing back tears of their own mixed with the gentle "click, click" of my godmother's camera capturing the moment. I turned the page over.

There will come a time in your life when temptation seems to be the only thing surrounding you. I pray that then, this

*promise ring will become more than a symbol to you . . .
that it will be a gentle reminder of God's love for you and
His purpose for creating you, and that it will remind you to
pray for wisdom and grace.*

*I promise I will love you forever,
Dad*

Looking up again, I saw that my parents' faces were as tear-drenched as my own. I opened the little black box. Nestled in the white leather interior was the petite promise ring. On either side of the golden band, three tiny diamonds led toward another small diamond encircled by four sapphires. We sat quietly together, taking in the magnitude of this gift.

Okay. My thoughts raced. *We've talked about the ancient Church teachings: God created sex to be a sign of His love within the bond of marriage. That's what my parents and my godmother and Deacon Ken say.* Making a promise to live that way seemed like a drastic leap, however. *What would this mean for me right now?*

The letter had asked me to pray for wisdom and grace. *Dear Jesus, Please give me the wisdom to know how to answer.*

Dreams of marriage and motherhood, which had come to a screeching halt the prior summer, echoed in my heart. Although hope had resurfaced by meeting Matt at the Planned Famine, other memories of sexual objectification still cut deeply. *Who should I believe?*

Mom and Dad? They think someone could care about me for who I am. I released a deep breath of relief. *If Mom and Dad's faith is true, then it makes sense to wait for whoever my future spouse might be.*

Suddenly, in light of the rest of my life, my Confirmation Crush seemed not so important. Lifting the ring from the case, I slid it onto my left hand. It looked beautiful.

A MAKESHIFT BUS STOP

Rockford, Michigan
Friday, June 14, 2002
Predawn

Like most West Michigan mornings, the air was heavy with humidity. I was among the first to arrive in Rockford for our youth group's departure for Franciscan University of Steubenville, Ohio. We were teaming with Our Lady of Consolation for the eight-hour bus ride down to the campus where we would convene with youth from the U.S. and Canada for a high-school youth conference. This would be my second time attending this conference.

With a theme of "Set Free," the three-day event would include sacraments, talks, skits, music with a full praise band, and lots of time to meet other Catholic high-school students. It was one of over a dozen conference sites hosted by Franciscan University. Tens of thousands of students would participate in these gatherings of faith over the course of the summer, in multiple cities. It was particularly exciting, coming on the heels of my confirmation.

This Steubenville weekend promised to be an exclamation mark on a school year of spiritual growth and deepening friendships. Between youth group, my confirmation, and my new promise ring, my experience of religion was increasingly filled with a deeply meaningful outlook on relationships. Many of my friends from other churches were planning to be there this particular weekend. *Including Matt.*

I had stayed in touch with Matt since that winter, when we met at the Planned Famine. We would chat on the computer over AOL Instant Messenger (or AIM) every few weeks. When friends signed in online, the box on the right of the computer screen would play a sound of an opening door. A list of screen names revealed who was available to chat.

My screen name was "EbonyAndIvory," and Matt's was "FaseRacer." Whenever I heard him log in, I would type a message to say hello. "FaseRacer" always seemed cheerful, and I was happy to learn he would be coming to Steubenville this year. *Matt's really funny and nice. Maybe we could become better friends!*

Waiting in the parking lot of OLC that morning, the sky was still dark. Dean Vernon was the kind of dad who made sure his daughter arrived early.

"Bye, Dad. Thanks for dropping me off."

"Bye, honey. Have a great weekend," my dad said, giving me a big kiss on the cheek. Then tears welled in the eyes of this intimidating, basketball-playing, gospel-music-singing mass of a man. Smiling widely, he nodded his head and said, "Be good."

"I will. Love you!"

Why do I always cry when my dad cries? My eyes followed him across the parking lot as he made his way back to our family van, stopping to give Deacon Ken a huge hug with ample slaps on the back. My dad was a school psychologist by trade, and he was also studying to become an ordained deacon. His excitement about Catholicism was as obvious as the prominent Green Bay Packer logo across his chest.

In a feeble attempt to block the cool morning breeze, I sat on the curb of the parking lot, hugging my knees. I was wearing jean shorts and a red tank top. *If Matt's been thinking about spending time with me again, we'll match!* A few more cars were arriving, with groggy-looking parents dropping off their teenagers. Some of the teens had been confirmed with me the month before.

I noticed one of the outgoing eighth-grade students from St. Francis arriving in a red car. *David Shaheen.* The tips of his spiky hair had been frosted blond for the summer, a la Backstreet Boys. Though my pride still stung, the whole Confirmation Crush incident seemed mostly comical now. *I'm over it.* I rolled my eyes and laughed at the silliness of teenage relationships.

Maybe Matt's on his way. Deacon Ken loaded large duffle bags into the massive motor coach.

A white sedan pulled up. Kevin jumped out from one side, and Ida shimmied down from the passenger seat. Waving to them, the jewels on my finger reflected the first rays of dawn. *Will Matt notice?* I looked more closely at the sapphires. I thought of my dad's tears and blinked back a couple more of my own.

Toying with the ring on my finger, I tried to ignore the goosebumps on my legs. *It's kind of cold for this outfit. Ohio is probably warmer, though.*

Then I saw Matt walking over.

As I had predicted, atop his slightly messy hair was the red visor. Over the past few months since we first met, however, I had wondered what he might look like when he got older. I didn't have to wonder anymore.

He's so much taller. Without warning, my heart began to slam inside my chest. *His shoulders are way broader than I remember them being. His freckles are so cute!* A rush of warmth spread over my cheeks. *What if he notices I'm blushing?*

Matt walked beside a stately looking man who must have been his father. Things seemed to move in slow motion. The man clasped Matt's arm once before departing.

From the beginning, Matt had inspired me to hope there was someone out there who could really care about me. *Maybe that someone is Matt!* Joyfulness was springing up deep inside me. It threatened to overflow, like a fountain filled to the brim.

Matt turned toward me with that same lighthearted smile from the Planned Famine. His eyes were shining with the innocent anticipation from our very first conversation. The fountain of joyfulness bubbled over within me, spreading a smile of unexpected elation across my face. I was savoring each second and dreaming of what was to come, all at once.

Matt broke the silence, anchoring the moment to reality. "Hi, Amanda," he said, in a resonating voice. The sun peeked around the church steeple. The future looked bright.

RED VISOR
MATT

Anna's House
Sunday, March 15, 2009
8:59 A.M.

A text came through on my phone. New message from Amanda Vernon. *Maybe she's canceling.*

"Hey Matt. I am on my way."

Perfect, she's running late. That's more my style.

"Still waiting?" the waitress asked.

"Yeah, but she's on her way. I just got a text from her. I'll keep waiting, but more coffee would be lovely."

She's driving here right now.

That thought brought to mind a time when I was driving to see her. Well, my dad was driving but that's where we were headed. It was a route he and I had taken many times, though this was the first time I met her there. I was on the cusp of many firsts, far more than I could imagine.

But of course, first there was breakfast.

REVELATIONS AND EGGS OVER EASY

Rockford, Michigan
Friday, June 14, 2002
Predawn

Through bleary eyes, I could see the pancakes and eggs piled high on my plate. For my dad, food equaled happiness. And so this great pile of a breakfast meant my dad was very happy for me.

Thanks for thinking of me, but I'm not awake enough to eat. But breakfast is the most important meal of the day. And it is going to be a very long day...and I do love all this food...and Dad is a good cook. I smiled at my plate and groggily started eating.

Dad stood at his usual place in front of the stove. The only light in our kitchen came from the overhead lights. *The sun isn't even up yet.* In typical fashion, Dad was alternating between his energetic singing and talking quickly about deep things. "This is going to be such a wonderful weekend for you, Matthew. It's got me thinking back to different retreats and conferences I've gone on," he said while flipping another serving of pancakes.

"How are the eggs?" he asked.

With mouth full and head mostly still full of sleep, I nodded my approval. Unrebuffed by my lack of response, he continued with an impromptu sermon. "In my prayer time the last few mornings, a theme keeps coming up." He looked down at the well-worn devotional book on the countertop.

I couldn't see the open page from where I sat, but I knew the margins were packed with his cramped writing and underlining, a date marking each inspiration. "It's Psalm thirty-seven, four. 'Find your delight in the Lord who will give you your heart's desire.' Isn't that exciting, Matthew? The Lord wants to give us our hearts' desires! What are the desires of your heart?"

My fork hovered halfway between my mouth and the plate as I tried to chew on both the pancakes and the deep question.

I only made progress on the pancakes.

"That's okay! Sometimes you don't even know what those desires are, at first. That's why it's so important to keep delighting in the Lord. Just really allow that joy to fill you up, especially at this conference, and he'll show you when the time is right. You're only going to get out of it what you put into it, though. So take some time to ask God what he wants to show you this weekend, okay?"

I do want to get a lot of out of this conference. That's good advice. As always.

Dad's advice and revelations continued as he ignored my protests and piled more eggs and pancakes onto my plate. *Well, they are really good.* The fork kept moving up and down. As the second helping was nearly gone and Dad threatened a third, the creaking stairs announced that Mom was awake. She walked into the kitchen, clutching her coffee cup as if to ward off the morning. "Good morning, my guys," she greeted the two of us. Her voice was even less awake than mine.

"MOM! You're awake! We're so glad you came down!" Dad exclaimed. His morning exuberance was unmatched.

"Not so loud, Steven, everyone else is still sleeping," Mom groaned as she leaned against him and added, "Thanks for bringing me coffee, love," with a smile.

Dad continued unabashed, "Your mom and I decided to take that verse seriously, about the desires of our hearts. We wrote this list of our deepest desires, right, Patty?"

Mom stared back, sleepy and unaware of the conversation she had just walked into. Looking out the window, where the first signs of dawn were emerging in the sky, she asked, "Isn't it getting late? Steven, you need to get Matt to church before he misses the bus."

"I know, but Matt wanted breakfast first!" came Dad's excuse, as he started clearing the dishes.

Mom stepped close and rubbed my back. "We're very proud of you, Eddie," she told me, shortening my middle name. "Going on this conference is a big decision. I know it might seem like a lot, but you'll have a great time. You'll pray and hear great talks and meet new people. You'll love it." She smiled reassuringly. *Mom's right. I will like it.*

"What am I saying?!" came Mom's sudden exclamation. "You need to go. Now. You'll be late!"

A MAKESHIFT BUS STOP

Friday, June 14, 2002
Daybreak

After a good breakfast and a last-minute rush to get in the car, I felt more awake. *Dad's right. I believe that God wants to give us our hearts' desires.* It wasn't something I'd spent a lot of time considering for myself, however. *I know a lot of times I have to do things I don't want to do—like getting up early today. I didn't want that. But I do want to go on this trip. Does that make it a desire of my heart?* I left the question hanging.

There was a lot to think about, and now that I would be starting high school at the end of the summer, I supposed I needed to start being a bit more thoughtful. And so I sat too tensely in the comfy leather passenger seat. It was a quick ten-minute drive from our house to the parish down the wide, four-lane boulevard. This early in the summer, the grass grew green and thick in the median. Eventually it would dry out and turn brown, but not yet.

I would be fifteen by the end of the month, and everything seemed to be picking up speed. Summer's end would bring high school. The two public middle schools funneled into one building with all five hundred or so freshman. Even this youth conference in Ohio was going to be a much bigger deal than the few local retreats I had attended in middle school. *But it's still going to be about Jesus. At least that's not different. Adoration, Mass, praise and worship.... Those things will be the same, right?*

Dad seemed to have noticed my anxiety as he sipped his coffee, waiting for the light to change. Perhaps in an effort to take my mind off the upcoming trip and what he presumed was concerning me, he teased as he often did, "You're not worrying about a girl, are you?"

"Ugh, no, Dad, come on!" I lied.

Well, I half-lied. I *was* nervous about the impending eight-hour trip in a bus full of people I barely knew, not to mention the weekend conference to follow. Both my junior-high youth director and older high-school students had raved about the Steubenville Youth Conference as a life-changing weekend. *Maybe it'll be just like the other retreats I've been on, but bigger.* The thought of an entire weekend with even more strangers, from all over the country, had me a little nervous. But more to the point, I was worried about seeing her again.

Since that first retreat, we had chatted on AIM, and so I knew she was going to be a part of the combined groups traveling down to Franciscan University of Steubenville. And although I had enjoyed our brief, intermittent chats, seeing each other for the second time was creating unexpected knots in the pit of my stomach.

The memory of my encounter with Christ on that middle-school retreat had lingered like a distant echo as the months passed. So it was with high hopes that I had signed up to attend this high-school youth conference. It seemed like a promising opportunity to tap into that kind of prayer and to meet God again in a way that was so real and so beautiful. But first, I had to figure out what I would do with myself upon seeing Amanda that morning. *What would she say? What should I say!?*

My dad must have sensed that his attempt to take my mind off things did not work. So he tried again.

"Well, Matt, this will be a great opportunity to pray about your vocation. You know Mom and I will always support you, no matter what. It's important to consider the priesthood too, and ask if that's where God is leading you."

"I know, Dad. I do." *Add that to the list of things to worry about.*

"If God's calling you to religious life, he'll put that desire on your heart. You remember what your mom and I told you at breakfast, right?"

"Yeah, Dad."

Although most of the people I knew from school were Protestant (Christian Reformed, to be specific), my parents normalized a Catholic identity in me from a young age. Receiving the sacraments was essential, along with prayer. They used words like "vocation" to mean "God's call" and spoke about "discernment" as a typical part of growing up and finding God's will.

My parents made it clear that an openness to religious life as a priest, a brother, or a sister was an important part of our family life. I also came to expect merciless teasing from my dad and older siblings if it seemed like I was too interested in any specific girls. I had talked to my mom about Amanda just enough to find out that my parents knew her parents from my dad's deacon program. I made sure to keep my feelings to myself, though. It was way less embarrassing that way.

Cutting into my silent musings again, my dad asked, "I see you're taking your new favorite visor with you. Do you think you'll get to wear it much during the conference?"

My dad's question made me realize I had started playing with my visor. I couldn't help thinking about her and that day we met whenever I saw it. As my dad pulled into the parking lot, I second-guessed my decision to wear the visor that morning. *What if she didn't still think the visor was cool? Or worse yet, what if she knew I wore it only because of her?*

Granted, she had mentioned sitting together on the bus ride. *Maybe she was only saying that to be nice. She probably forgot all about it by now.*

My dad parked the car. We walked across the parking lot toward the other teens and their tired-looking parents. I dropped my duffle bag and my pillow in the accumulating mound of luggage. With his hand on my shoulder, my dad and I said our goodbyes. "Remember: the desires of your heart, right?" he said, before turning and walking back toward the car.

Looking around, that stupid visor regretfully perched atop my head, I saw Amanda was already there. She was wearing jean shorts with a red tank top, and her hair was styled in long, thin braids. As I walked toward her, her face lit up in a warm smile. Bright, straight teeth flashed in the morning sun.

"Hi, Amanda," I said. Blessedly, my treacherous voice didn't crack. It had been doing that far too much lately.

"Hi, Matt. How's it going?" Amanda greeted me, standing up energetically.

"Great! It's early, but I'm stoked for the trip."

She smiled again. "Me too! Nice visor, by the way," she added.

"Oh! Well . . ." *Just don't say anything stupid.*

Tilting her head toward the bus, she asked, "Did you want to sit together?"

"Definitely," I answered with a grin. It was, certainly, a very nice visor. And I knew that it was going to be a very good trip.

Freshman Year

Verse 1

We're talking for hours about whatever
I'm thinking 'bout your last name
Dreaming 'bout forever
We don't have a care
I'm just playing with your hair

Chorus

Welcome to my league
It's a whole new speed
Join the club
Have no fear
Fall in love
Freshman year

Verse 2

My friends say you like me
I think that just might be
But you're so hard to read
Maybe 'cause you're fifteen
You're invited to the cool kids' team
Come on up and sit with me

Bridge

I'm so glad you're here
You've made it to your freshman year
You'll have so much fun ahead
If girls like me don't mess with you instead
Hey, I'm learning just like you
Only I make it look cool
I feel those butterflies inside
Why're you looking at me like you're surprised?
I got my tan skin, skinny braids, strong voice, and a heart full of dreams
I'm starin' atcha darin' ya to try and keep up with me

SET FREE
AMANDA

Grand Rapids, Northeast side
Sunday, March 15, 2009
9:05 A.M.

If I drive just a bit over the speed limit I won't keep Matt waiting too long. Along the expressway, the sun shone warmly through the moonroof. *Kinda sunny for March. Perfect. 'Cause warmth equals happiness.*

Summertime was my favorite of Michigan's distinct four seasons. Summer was always warm, and carefree, and a time to dream. My siblings and I spent hours swimming and running along the sand dunes at Lake Michigan. Other glorious summertime memories blossomed out of various youth group excursions and retreats.

Turning off the highway, I stopped at the intersection and waited for the light to change. I thought gratefully of those Steubenville Youth Conferences, where I heard testimonies from teens and adults alike—plus stories of saints—who entrusted their entire lives to God. Giving myself to God like they did sounded exciting, but also intimidating. And yet, standing shoulder to shoulder with friends made it not so scary.

Driving away from the highway, toward breakfast, I let out a nostalgic sigh. *Standing next to Matt was exciting, no matter what. But especially when we were facing the prospect of the rest of our lives.*

ON CAMPUS

Steubenville, Ohio
Friday, June 14, 2002
After dark

The air was warm and humid the night Matt and I first walked around Franciscan University together. Fields of deep, dewy grass and plots of colorful flowers filled in the spaces between the various school buildings, from the John Paul II Library, to the bookstore, to the Portiuncula chapel with twenty-four-hour Eucharistic adoration. Just over twenty-two hundred college students were enrolled at the university, but this weekend, high-school students filled the dorms. The main events of the youth conference took place in the large fieldhouse. After hours, we were free to spread out around campus.

Lamplight illuminated the walkways. Some students gathered around picnic benches, others played basketball. One group threw a glow-in-the-dark Frisbee back and forth on the nearest lawn terrace.

Many of the teens wore matching T-shirts to distinguish their youth group. A couple of groups touted the adage "NO PURPLE" across the front of their shirts, with the boys wearing blue and the girls wearing pink. It was, in my opinion, an obnoxious way of promoting chastity. *No blending our colors? Well, within reason, obviously.*

The red visor snugly circled my long, micro braids. *I feel those same bubbly, carefree feelings from the night of the Planned*

Famine. Except now, Matt's a freshman. And he's totally dat-able. What should I do with this? We had spent almost an hour strolling and laughing around the school grounds.

Maybe I'll try a more serious question. "What do you think of your first Steubenville Conference?"

"Man, everything has been great so far! The music, the talks—really inspiring. The downtime has been fun too, play-ing hacky sack and stuff. Fantastic. I like it." Matt looked up into the night sky.

Emotionally charged liturgies and talks were customary at Steubenville. *Surprisingly, Matt fits right in.* Unlike Matt, many clearly took a while to warm up to it. High-energy worship was commonplace at St. Francis, though. My dad had introduced gospel music to our church choir, so our liturgies were always filled with tight harmonies and driving rhythms. Clapping, hands raised high, and crying during the homily—these hall-marks of our weekly Sunday Mass weren't typical for Catholic churches in the United States.

I inquired further. "Is faith a pretty big thing for your family? Do you guys have this kind of music and prayer pretty often?"

"Well, we always talk about faith at home," Matt responded.

"Same. To say the least." *In fact, my dad begins conversations with, "Here's what the Holy Spirit revealed to me today," almost every day.*

"It is really cool to hear a thousand kids from different parts of the world singing together," I said. "Oh! Did you meet the girls from Toronto earlier? We took a picture together. They were car-rying a Canadian flag, which matched my shirt and your visor."

"That part is really cool. You're right," Matt agreed.

"The visor?"

"Obviously the visor," Matt quipped. "And seeing everyone from all over. I usually hang out with people from, well, Rock-ford. Or our family goes to our cabin up north. So this is new."

"Oh, the ultra-cosmopolitan suburb of Rockford. How could I forget?" I adjusted the visor on my forehead, throwing him a half-smile.

"Hey!" Matt shot back in stride. "There will be like five hundred students at my school this year. And that's just the Freshman Center. Right off the bat I won't even have a chance to know half of them. How many did you say are in your class?" Matt tapped his chin.

"Not fair." *He's making me laugh again! He also does have a valid point.* "Well, at least I'm always first in every subject." I whipped my braids around for dramatic effect.

"Congratulations! You're also last, though, so there's that too." He shrugged, gazing up at the sky again with a smile. *I can't outwit this kid. He's good. I'm all out of replies, besides laughter.*

"How do you like being homeschooled?" Matt asked. "Do you get to stay in your pajamas all day?" His tone was still teasing, but his expression displayed genuine curiosity now. *Since when do guys care about my thoughts or feelings? Just take a chill pill and answer the question, Amanda.*

Matt nodded as he listened to my description of a typical school day and how the flexibility allowed me to focus on my love of music. We walked in pace with each other comfortably, side by side. *He's keeping pretty quiet. Is he interested in this? What about the fact that guys only pay attention because they want some sort of payoff?*

Glancing over at me briefly from the corner of his eye, Matt kept walking. After a few minutes of unbroken silence, I gathered my thoughts. *I'm being too deep. Time to lighten the mood.* "It's either write songs and reflect on life, or go outside and entertain my little siblings all day. So I reflect a lot."

Matt laughed again and then pointed out that we were near the women's residence hall. *Wow, we've circled the campus three times, but I didn't realize we were here already.* Playfully whipping the visor off, I tossed it in his direction, flipping my braids back into place.

Though Matt's hand shot out to snag the visor, his eyes were on me. *Good catch.* Matt studied my face for a moment. The freckles across his nose were just barely visible in the lamplight. Suspicion crept up again. *Did he think all this talking would lead to making out? I wonder if he's been thinking about kissing me.* Guarded excitement surged like electric sparks inside me. Kissing sounded like a surprisingly good idea. *But not if he only likes me for my body, though.*

Matt held the visor back out. "Keep it for the weekend?" he asked. We shared a smile. He laid it in my open hands and walked away.

VOCATIONS CALL

Sunday, June 16, 2002
Midmorning

By the final day of the Steubenville Youth Conference, all of the attendees had been through a lot of intense prayer, and it was time to celebrate. We all gathered in the fieldhouse that Sunday morning for our triumphant send-off. There was one more call to action to be navigated, however, before heading back to our homes.

A popular ceremony at many youth retreats, the vocations call made my pulse race in fear.

I found the religious life of priests, brothers, sisters, and nuns to be inspiring, but only from a distance. *"Love demands a response,"* was a quote I had heard from one such nun, St. Thérèse of Lisieux. Recognized as a Doctor of the Church, St. Thérèse was one of the most celebrated exemplars of living the Catholic Faith. She only lived from 1873 to 1897, and yet she made a lasting impact in her short twenty-four years through her prayers, writing, and her ardent belief that *"God would not inspire unattainable desires."*

I was inspired by stories such as hers but scared to even ask the question whether the Lord might be calling me to that life.

This time, Fr. Stan Fortuna took the stage in his hooded gray habit. He was a rapping, streetwise priest with a New York accent. Silver streaks ran through his well-trimmed beard and his dark ponytail. "If you've ever considered that you might be called to the religious life, please come on down to the front of the altar," his melodic voice called out into the mic.

"Maybe this is something that's been on your mind, or maybe it's coming up for the first time." *It only comes up when my parents mention it . . . on a monthly basis.* During our family Rosary, my dad always adapted this special prayer for each of the Vernon children:

> "Lord, we ask you to bless Amanda, keep her holy
> and pure all the days of her life. We ask that if she
> is to be a nun, she would say 'yes' the very first time
> you call her name. If she is to be married someday,
> please bless whatever young man is out there. Keep
> him holy and pure all the days of his life."

All the kids giggled whenever he got to the part about the "young man" out there somewhere.

Fr. Stan's voice called me back to attention. "Here's another question. Have you ever thought about *not* becoming a priest or a brother or a sister? If so, please come on down." *Well of course I've thought about not becoming a religious.* With reluctance, I stood up. *And now all one thousand of us will do the same.*

Not even one hundred kids stood. But Matt did.

Together with the other 10% of the crowd, we walked down from the bleachers to stand at the base of the large stage, converted with an altar for Mass. *I just don't want to be down here right now. Is everyone going to think I want to be a nun?* As Fr. Stan prayed over us, I tried not to be hard-hearted. *Lord, help me to be open to Your call, whatever it is.*

After the prayer, Fr. Stan recommended we talk about this moment with a mentor in the faith. *No, no, no. No way. Okay maybe. But probably not.*

"Last of all," he said, "I'ma teach you a prayer. 'Holy Spirit, command me to do Your will.'

I must warn you, however. These are dangerous words. You pray this prayer, the Lord will answer. So prepare yourself. Your life is about to be transformed. You ready?"

I'm ready. Not ready to ask a mentor about joining the convent. I will pray, though, right now. Holy Spirit, command me to do Your will.

Cheering filled the fieldhouse. Tentatively, I surveyed the glowing faces of the students beside me. Then Matt's eyes locked with mine. He smiled down with an overflowing radiance. *There's that look again, like he can see my soul.*

Matt held my gaze, beaming ever more joyfully until the applause died down. *If Matt is so overjoyed at the prospect of following God's call, why shouldn't I answer boldly too?*

Heading back to our seats, my heart was a little less afraid.

I'M JUST PLAYING WITH YOUR HAIR

Ohio Turnpike
Sunday, June 16, 2002
Evening

Matt and I sat together on the bus ride back to Michigan. From the aisle side of the smooth, plasticky seat, I intermittently jumped up to talk with other kids or to lead a song from the front microphone. After our bus had covered a couple of hundred miles, Ida asked to join us.

"Let a girl in, would ya?" she insisted with her typical sass.

Matt hopped nimbly down to sit in front of us, and I slid over to take the window seat. Ida grabbed my hand for assistance before assuming the aisle spot. Even in the cramped floor space, Matt was able to stretch out, since Ida's shorter legs didn't reach the ground. Although I tucked my feet back to give Matt the most room possible, my tan legs were now immediately in front of his chest.

Well, I did hint to Matt earlier about playing with his hair.

Ida was already chatting up a storm. "Whew, did you see those boys from Jersey? The one with the backwards hat? Mmm! He was fine. You people might go on retreats to pray, but I'm here to pray *and* to admire God's work. You know what I'm saying?" *We know what you're saying, Chiquita.*

I ran my left hand through Matt's light-brown hair. He grinned and closed his eyes. *Whoa, soft! I've never felt hair like this before. Sometimes my little brothers' fresh buzz cuts feel smooth, but even then, their fibers are pretty coarse.* Matt blinked and started teasing Ida about her Steubenville weekend. "So you had vocational discernment in mind, Ida? The kind that starts with an 'M' and rhymes with 'Jerry, a boy from New Jersey?'"

For the next couple of hours, I talked with Ida, laughed at Matt's jokes, and moved my fingers back and forth through his super-soft hair. Eventually, Deacon Ken's voice sounded on the overhead speakers. "Students, we're approaching Lansing, Michigan. We'll be back in Rockford in under two hours!"

"I'm gonna miss you, Matt," I said. *This is your cue to tell me we should see each other sometime soon.*

"I'm gonna miss you too," he said, looking up at me. Chiquita promptly called us out of the moment before he could say any more.

"Matt! Your youth director is heading this way." A look of panic crossed Matt's face. *What's the problem?* He frantically requested the pillow I'd been using as an armrest. Skeptically, I handed it over. Pulling his legs back against his chest and ducking his head underneath the pillow, he disappeared from sight.

"Hi, ladies, how are you?" Mrs. Buehler asked.

"Oh hi, Mrs. Buehler! Doing great. Thanks for asking. I think there are some more Rockford students farther back," I said confidently. *It's not a lie.*

Chiquita, nodding slowly, was silent for once.

"Okay, enjoy the rest of the trip. We'll be home soon."

"Thanks!" Holding my breath, Mrs. Buehler walked toward the back of the motor coach. *Well, Matt clearly doesn't want to be seen sitting at my knees. I wasn't thinking of this as something wrong. Was he?* Matt peered out from behind the pillow. Ida and Matt laughed nervously together after he let out a monumental sigh and said, "Whew, that was close."

What just happened? It dawned on me that Mrs. Buehler might've suspected something more than simply messing with Matt's hair had she seen him seated at my feet. I knew I was being flirtatious, but I hadn't imagined it was anything to get in trouble for. *Shoot. Why is Matt doing anything with me that he feels we need to hide? Is this my fault?*

"You'd better get up, Matt," I said. "What if she stops again on her way back?"

Chiquita rolled her eyes. "Guess I'll move, then. My bad," she said sarcastically. Stepping down into the aisle, she released my arm as she gained her balance.

This is a little confusing. Matt's definitely interested in me. But he's also embarrassed? As I slid back to the aisle seat, Matt hopped up next to the window. *I also totally want to spend more time together, but he hasn't thrown out any ideas. And now he's acting scared. Looks like this'll be up to me.*

Chapter 3

SET FREE
MATT

Anna's House
Sunday, March 15, 2009
9:06 A.M.

The coffee was good, fresh, strong. The cup of cream remained untouched on the table, as did the sugar. *Why mess with a good thing?*

The sun was shining, blazing bright on the piles of dirtying snow at the edges of the parking lot. *Too bad winter is almost over. I'll miss the cold and the snow.*

Each of the seasons brings its own beauty and style. While winter was my favorite, I enjoyed parts of them all. *I suppose I do have some good summer memories.*

Punctuating my most plentiful summer recollections (mainly camping and exploring the outdoors up north), Steubenville Conferences stood out as mountaintop experiences of faith and conviction. Those peaks were glorious and thrilling, but mountaintops are not meant to be camped on. *Peter was among the first to get that one wrong.* So as beautiful as it was up there, and after all of that effort, we always had to retrace our steps down. The memory and the experience remained.

Of course, mountain climbing is all the more fun when you enjoy the company.

ON CAMPUS

Steubenville, Ohio
Friday, June 14, 2002
After dark

It was still muggy in Steubenville, even though the sun had already set on Franciscan University. The darkness brought some reprieve, though the continued humidity meant that I was still perspiring. *At least she can't see me sweating with just the lamp light.*

There were groups of teens here and there about campus, either sitting and talking or playing some game. *Cool! Glow-in-the-dark Frisbee. But I don't know those guys, and hopefully Amanda will want to go around another lap. I wonder how many times we've circled?*

This wasn't just small talk anymore. We were well past that. We were discussing meeting people from all over and about the differences of my school versus hers. I grinned as another homeschool joke was rewarded. Another laugh! With this one turning into giggles. *Keep it rolling.*

"How do you like being homeschooled? Do you get to stay in your pajamas all day?" No laugh this time. *Oh well, listening to her talk about something she loves, which appears to be most things, is just as nice.*

"It's awesome. My mom actually does expect me to get dressed every morning before breakfast and family prayer. Because there's so much flexibility, I can structure the schoolwork however I'd like for the rest of the day." *Makes sense.*

"My parents let us focus more on whichever subjects are most appealing to each of us. So that means I get to write tons of music." We kept walking. *What would that be like? If my folks did that, I can't imagine how long it would take to get my brother, Steve, out of bed. Plus, that seems like way too much freedom. But then I could play out in the woods in the middle of the day. What subject would I choose to study? Natural science maybe. That would give me an excuse to be outside more. But who would teach me?*

"Umm . . ." Amanda said as the interior warning bells rang. *Oops, focus. She'll think I'm being rude. Is she annoyed with me?*

Very slyly, I glanced from the corner of my eye to see if she was. *Crap crap crap, she caught me! Now she knows how self-conscious I am. But she's not making fun of me for it. And we are still walking together.* Amanda continued. She wasn't being defensive, just honest. *Close one.*

Our strolling continued, as did our talking and laughter. Too soon, though, I realized we had come back around to the women's dorm. That reminded me, I needed to be back at my own.

"One of the youth leaders wanted the Rockford guys to meet up before turning in tonight. So I'd better head to the men's dorm. This is your place, right?"

Playfully whipping the visor off, she tossed it to me. It was a graceful motion that not only returned the visor but also flipped her braids out around her and then back into place. *She's good at that.* Amanda looked back at me. Light from a nearby lantern graced one side of her face, its shadows accentuating the arc of her eyebrows and the gentle curve of her lips. Even with her face half lit in the lamplight, the beauty mark above her mouth drew me in. I didn't want to walk away, yet I didn't know what else to do either.

The Steubenville speaking team had announced a popular idiom: no purple! In a nutshell, if blue represents boys, and pink represents girls, well, mixing those colors would be against the rules of the youth conference. The idea was clear: no physical intimacy.

I suppose there's one thing I could do. I held the visor back out. "Keep it for the weekend?" I asked.

We shared a smile, and she let me lay that awesome visor back in her open hands.

VOCATIONS CALL

Sunday, June 16, 2002
Midmorning

After spending Friday evening and all day Saturday with a thousand other teens, Sunday morning of the conference had an exultant air of celebration. Congregating again in the field-house, where we had heard talks, gone to adoration, and sung until our vocal chords were sore, this was our departing session before the closing Mass.

"Let's make some noise for the final session of our conference! How's everyone feeling?!" I hollered a response back to the emcee with the rest of the kids who were not too groggy from the previous night's intense adoration session. "I can't hear you! Did you say you're feeling blessed?" This time, just about everybody joined in. *How could you not feel blessed right now?*

"Before Mass begins, we'll take some moments to reflect on how God is calling you! What's your specific path to growing in happiness and holiness?"

With that, Fr. Stan Fortuna, the only priest I'd ever seen rap and a fireball of a Franciscan friar from the Bronx, took the stage. "If you've ever considered that you might be called to the religious life, please come on down to the front of the altar." I had witnessed a few of these invitations before. Each time there had been an honest voice in me saying, *God might be calling me to the priesthood.* Standing up to admit that in front of everyone always seemed so high pressure, though. *They'll all be looking at me, and what if they don't think I'm called.*

"Maybe this is something that's been on your mind, or maybe it's coming up for the first time," Fr. Stan continued. *There is that honest voice again. It's not the first time.*

"Here's another question. Have you ever thought about *not* becoming a priest or a brother or a sister? If so, please come on down." *Well, of course I had thought about not becoming a religious. I'm thinking about not answering the call right now.* That simple turn of phrase seemed to take the edge off. *I have thought about not being a priest or a brother. I can come forward for that.*

I stood up. So did Amanda.

Along with about a hundred other teens, we walked down from the bleachers to the front, where the songs, talks, prayers, and Mass took place. Amanda and I stood side by side at the foot of the altar.

"All right, all right, all right. Here we go. Are you listening? Not to me, but to the Spirit. We're gonna pray together right now," spouted Fr. Stan, with the same wild energy he poured into everything. He extended his arms over us. He prayed an earnest plea for God's blessing, courage, and direction to stir in our hearts.

Bowing, I let Fr. Stan's words wash over me. There was something solemn in that moment. His poetic prayer did not seem foolish, nor his actions empty. There was a weight behind his words, a deep truth pressing on my heart. My dad's words came back to mind: "If God's calling you to religious life, he'll put that desire on your heart." In that truth was joy.

"Amen," Fr. Stan concluded.

"Amen," I grinned.

"Now, some direction! When you go back home, you cannot simply forget about this moment. You need to take some action. Talk to one of your leaders about this. Ask someone you trust from church to pray with you about the possibility of religious life." *Makes sense, but who?*

To conclude, Fr. Stan taught us a prayer to the Holy Spirit, with the caveat that praying it would, indeed, transform our lives. *Awesome. I am ready. I'm not sure what for, but yeah, I feel ready for whatever the Lord wants for me. Holy Spirit, command me to do Your will.*

"Will you join me in commending these brave young people for their courage this morning?" A thunderous applause arose from the people who had stayed put. *There are a lot more people still in their seats.* I looked around at the students who had gathered. *This is good.* I smiled. *I don't know what this means for us, but you can't go wrong by trusting in the Lord.* I caught Amanda's eye and grinned wider. *If she's up here too, then it's not foolish.*

Heading back to our seats, my heart was full. *I don't know where God is calling me, but I intend to listen.*

I'M JUST PLAYING WITH YOUR HAIR

Ohio Turnpike
Sunday, June 16, 2002
Evening

Amanda sat next to me on the drive home from Steubenville. We had spent pretty much all of our free time together that weekend. Since we wouldn't see each other much after the weekend ended, it was best to make the most of the ride back.

I sat in the window seat. *Beautiful scenery on one side, a beautiful girl on the other. This'll be a very nice eight hours.*

Amanda's energetic joy didn't lessen even as the rolling hills of Southeastern Ohio flattened out into the bland fields of the

Turnpike. She was constantly jumping up to chat with different people or lead the entire bus in our favorite songs over the PA system. All the while, she was smiling and laughing, in that way of hers that made everyone smile and laugh right along.

Shortly after we crossed the Michigan border, Ida made her way over.

"Let a girl in, would you?" she demanded with more sass than her small frame could bear.

In order to make ample room for the three of us, and since I had been sitting in that same position for hours, I slid nimbly down to sit on the floor with my back against the cool side of the bus. Amanda shifted over next to the window, and Ida climbed into the aisle seat.

Amanda's darkly tanned legs came down just in front me. The hot summer temperatures meant that all of us were in shorts. *Well, this is more exciting than I thought. I was just looking for a way to stretch my legs, but the view is even better from here!*

Amanda let her left hand fall easily onto the top of my head, and she started playing with my hair. *Good thing I took a shower this morning!* My hair was very soft when it was that clean. Amanda seemed impressed.

The next couple of hours passed with laughing, teasing, and Amanda absently running her fingers through my hair. Even though the hard floor became much less comfortable, everything else about the arrangement was quite pleasant. *I like this.* Yet I questioned how closely we were adhering to the "no purple" rule. If her wide smile and easy laughter were any indication, Amanda felt uninhibited about this particular display of affection. *If she's fine playing with my hair like this, it's okay with me.*

Every once in a while, when Amanda would rest her left hand on her knee at my eyeline, I would study the petite, gold ring on her finger. The deep blue stones and small diamonds were beautiful to look at. Even more admirable than how it looked on her hand was the promise she made to go along with it. On the ride down to Steubenville, Amanda had explained about the ring her father had given her, and how it was a sign of saving her virginity for marriage. *It's amazing how she shares her faith so openly, even about such personal stuff.*

Eventually, Deacon Ken's voice sounded on the overhead speakers. "Students, we're approaching Lansing, Michigan. We'll be back in Rockford in under two hours!"

"I'm gonna miss you, Matt," Amanda said, looking down at me with a soft smile.

"I'm gonna miss you too," I replied. *I wish I could see her more often. The next retreat isn't until the fall.*

Ida cut into the moment. "Matt! Your youth director is heading this way." *Crap crap crap crap.*

"What!? Right now?" I asked, as panic replaced the sense of excitement I had been opening up to.

"It seems like she's just talking to the Rockford kids. She's about five rows away," Amanda said calmly.

I can't let anyone see me! Everything about this position is "purple"! My head, her legs, her hand in my hair, my feelings.... "Give me your pillow!" It was the only thing near us that could possibly conceal me.

"What? Why?" Amanda asked, seeming to miss the importance of not letting anyone know I was this close to her. *This'll definitely get us in trouble. The teasing would never stop.*

"Just give me your pillow, okay?" *Surely that would keep me covered enough so that Mrs. Buehler wouldn't see me this comfortable with Amanda.*

Amanda held out the pillow she'd been using as an armrest. I snagged it swiftly and ducked underneath it. After pulling my legs back from the aisle, I ought to have disappeared completely from a passing glance. *I'm just some bags and a pillow at*

Amanda's feet. Not a teenage boy enjoying the proximity of a cute girl. And definitely not making purple.

I kept still as Amanda and Ida made small talk with Mrs. Buehler. After what felt like an hour, Mrs. Buehler moved down the aisle.

"Thanks!" I whispered, still afraid of being seen. "Whew, that was close." I breathed a sigh of relief as my heart still hammered in my chest.

What would I have done if Mrs. Buehler had seen me? She definitely would've guessed how interested I am in Amanda. She would've thought I was breaking the rules—the rules put there specifically to help us on the retreat. That would've been mortifying.

"You'd better get up, Matt. What if she stops on her way back?" Amanda said. *Good call.*

Thankfully Ida chimed in. "Guess I'll move, then. My bad." She gripped Amanda's arm for balance as she stepped down. "Hey, Kevin! You saved me some of those Hot Cheetos, right?!" *I hope her shouts don't draw attention.*

I hopped back up into the window seat after Amanda slid to the aisle. I looked out the dark window as the scattered lights moved past. *Being that close was really nice. It'd be great if we could stay close. But it almost got me in so much trouble.*

More Life

Verse 1

When we first met, you wore that red sun visor
Somehow you made me rethink everything
You never stopped making me wiser
Challenging my views, 'cause it's always like new

Chorus

With you, colors burn brighter
With you, my heart beats harder
With you, I have more strife
I have more joy, I have more life

Verse 2

When we first met, I took you by surprise
I opened your eyes to brand new possibilities
I never stopped making you wiser
Challenging your views, 'cause it's always like new

Bridge

My life was calmer without you
My life was simpler without you
My life had less to resolve
Less problems to solve, without you
Don't you worry, I'll never let you go
With you my life is just so full
And without me, where would you be?
Your life would be less demanding
Your life would be less outstanding
Your life would be less frustrating, less irritating, without me
Your life would be less confusing, your life would be so much less moving
Good thing you're choosing
Life abundantly

Chapter 4

BIG TENT AND BARE TRUTH
AMANDA

Parking lot of Anna's House
Sunday, March 15, 2009
9:10 A.M.

At the peak of the modest cement structure, nestled under its deeply slanted roof, hung the sign "ANNA'S HOUSE." Pulling up next to the building, I shifted into park. Lifting a tube of clear lip gloss from my purse, I dropped the mirror down from above the driver's seat.

Deep emotion churned in my chest, replacing the butterflies that had accompanied the drive over. *What is this feeling?* A smile crinkled around the edges of the eyes looking back in the mirror, as I recalled the weekend with Matt that set a new course for my life. *It must be gratitude.*

As a fifteen-year-old, there was a widening disconnect between my convictions about faith and love, and my inward motivation. Through my affection for Matt, my own intentions came into clearer focus. *I'm so grateful for how I was able to finally see myself.*

Applying a final swipe of lip gloss, I closed the mirror. Sometimes, seeing your own reflection calls for some adjustments.

IS HE YOUR BOYFRIEND?

Steubenville, Ohio
June 21, 2003
Midmorning

A full year had passed since Matt and I first walked around campus together at Franciscan University. Although my budding hopes for music were starting to blossom, I hadn't seen Matt nearly as often as I had hoped. Our distance hadn't kept me from thinking of him.

A photo taken of Matt and me at last summer's conference was tacked to the corkboard beside my bed. When I woke up in the morning and when I lay down to sleep at night, I looked at the two of us, sitting close together on one of the sprawling lawns, smiling in the sunlight. Our matching orange T-shirts from St. Francis and OLC youth groups stood out against the grass behind us, like the contrast of my tan legs next to Matt's fair skin. *My heart held so many hopes that day.*

I had disclosed some of those hopes to my parents that fall. "Amanda, what do you want to do with your life?" my dad had asked gregariously, seemingly out of the blue. *Classic Dean Vernon style.*

"I really want to do music and to use it for ministry."

My dad had replied reassuringly, "Well, if music ministry is God's will for you, God will open the door and you'll just have to walk right through. And your mom and I will be right behind you."

Within a month of that talk with my dad, Deacon Ken approached me after a youth group night at St. Francis. "Amanda, how would you like to record a CD?" he asked. "We could pay for it with our youth group budget and set up a concert for you to share the music in ministry at a big youth rally."

REALLY??!! I already have a dozen songs written and ready to go! ARE YOU SERIOUS?! I mean, "Yeah, that'd be great!"

So, with my parents' help, I recorded ten songs at an audio studio and commissioned a local artist to paint a photo of me for the cover. We ordered a thousand copies for the first run. *Volume discount!* My dad tells the story of loading the boxes of CDs into our basement, asking himself, "What are we doing to do with all of these?" He didn't have to wait long for an answer. Soon after the debut of my CD, concert requests began rolling in from churches around Grand Rapids, and even across Michigan.

Undoubtedly, the doors for music were wide open. But with Matt? We had only seen each other *once* since the last Steubenville Conference. *At least he was at the fall retreat in Grand Rapids with the OLC youth group.* With the exception of that one weekend, we kept in touch over AIM when he logged on intermittently. Whenever I invited Matt to come into Grand Rapids, he said he was busy with his family.

And yet, at our second Steubenville Conference together, Matt and I fell back into step with each other in an instant. Walking around campus that warm summer morning felt effortless and exhilarating at once. *Maybe the door that's been closed with Matt is about to open!* I had given a concert as part of the fall retreat, and Matt seemed genuinely impressed.

"Do you think you'll do music for a career?" Matt was asking. *After so many months apart, he still looks at me with so much admiration and respect.*

"That'd be a dream come true. What about you? Will you be a professional actor someday? I've seen your improv skills! Plus, the Rockford kids keep mentioning your acting abilities." *In fact, Robin's here this weekend.*

Robin was the female lead from Matt's high-school play, and an outgoing senior. Rumor had it, the two of them shared an onstage kiss. *Matt kissing anyone else?* A knot of jealousy twisted in the pit of my stomach. *I hope he doesn't bring it up.*

"Well, my dad works in real estate, so I might sell houses someday. Besides, my dad says that actors are either ugly or gay."

Finally, an opportunity to let him know how cute I think he is! "And you're neither." I tossed out the compliment.

"Well, I know I'm not ugly," Matt said jovially.

He's joking, right? Or is that the reason he hasn't accepted any of my invites to come see me at the St. Francis youth group? Maybe he's not interested in me like that after all.

"Hey! Is he your boyfriend?" I turned to see who had shouted. A husky teen smirked in my direction.

In a split second, a familiar succession of rapid-fire reactions blazed through my mind.

Curiosity. *Who's yelling?*

Realization. *He's looking straight at me.*

Appreciation. *He must think I'm cute.*

Indignation. *He's looking at me as if I'm a collection of body parts.*

Strategy. *How to get away without causing a scene?*

Fear. *If he's starting out this aggressively, will he get violent?*

Cynicism. *That's just the way guys are.*

"Hey! Girl! Is he your boyfriend, or what?" he shouted again.

Finally, a glimmer of hopefulness. *On the bright side, this is a prime opportunity for Matt to stand up for me.*

"Hey! Well . . ." I looked at Matt expectantly, giving him permission to answer first.

"No!" Matt shook his head back and forth quickly. "No, no . . . ." *Either he's really nervous, or he really doesn't like the sound of being my boyfriend.* With a grimace, I thought again of Matt's words. *"Actors are either ugly or gay."*

"If this clown's not your boyfriend, then who is?" The boy's attempt at flattery abrasively cut through my ruminating. Resentment brimmed around my lips.

"I don't have a boyfriend. Thanks for asking, but we're gonna keep walking now."

"When you change your mind, how will I know? Unless I get your number?" *Would he step off already? I wish Matt would help me out here.*

"I don't give my number to guys I've just met." In an attempt to diffuse the boy's indignant body language, I swiftly flashed a smile. "I'm honored you asked, really. But Matt and I are heading to meet our groups soon. So we'd better get going. See you around."

With a firm nudge to Matt's shoulder, I pivoted in the opposite direction and quickly picked up the pace. Matt followed along.

"You know, you could just say 'yes,'" I said.

"What do you mean?"

Walking even faster, I checked whether we were being followed. We weren't. "If some guy's harassing me. You could just say you're my boyfriend."

"Oh!" Matt's eyes widened. "Okay! Yeah, next time." *Maybe he **is** gay.*

CONFESSION

June 21, 2003
Afternoon

"Would you care for an examination of conscience?" Later that sunny afternoon, a teen volunteer distributed booklets to those of us standing in the outdoor line for confession. I accepted with a smile.

A gigantic tent stretched across a sprawling field of green in the middle of Franciscan University. Pairs of folding chairs were scattered underneath the tent. Dozens of priests sat patiently as students and adult chaperones continually filed through. *Perfect time to go to confession for the month.*

The examination of conscience was a printed page of blue construction paper. At the top, there was a synopsis of confession. *This is nothing new to me.* I had been going to confession about once a month since I first received the sacrament in second grade, before my First Communion. I had learned that it was a graced moment to ask God's mercy for the times I had turned away from Him. That every time I sinned, I wounded the Body of Christ because we're all connected as one family in faith. And that confession also reconciled me with the entire Church.

Farther down the blue page were questions about my relationship with God, others, and myself. I was almost through reading the questions when my eyes caught on the line, "Have you purposefully exchanged words, glances, or touches with another, or with yourself, to sexually arouse?" I paused.

A memory came to mind from Mass that morning. While a thousand other high-school students listened to the homily, I was focused on Matt seated next to me. He was listening intently when I let my leg slide over to rest against his. To an onlooker, my demeanor had said, "We're at Mass. We're praying. Everything is cool." Internally? *Hallelujah!* Cue the gospel choir singing Handel's *Messiah.*

My heartbeat quickened as the confession line grew shorter. *It's not bad to be excited about someone I like so much.* I felt an unwelcome knot in the pit of my stomach. *I did that because . . . because I care about Matt. I was just showing him that by . . . turning him on in the middle of Mass?* Emitting a slight groan, I wrestled with the truth.

I meant to stir up specific feelings in myself, and I wanted Matt to feel the same. Can you blame a girl for trying? Besides, controlling the chemistry between us makes me feel powerful, and wanted. So . . . maybe I was using him.

Only two people were ahead in line now. *I'm a touchy-feely person. I have an Italian mom, after all! And I'm wearing a promise ring! I'm not planning to have sex! That doesn't rule out the possibility of using other people to boost my own self-esteem, though. I also know, deep down, there's a difference between showing someone I care, and using my body to control another person.*

"You may go on in now. Choose any open seat," said the teen volunteer. I didn't feel so great about what I needed to say anymore.

Selecting a plastic folding chair beside a young priest, I sat down timidly, still grasping the blue construction paper in my left hand. The priest wore a white robe called an alb, under a purple stole (a long strip of fabric, like an open scarf). Gesturing with open palms, he said, "Let's begin, in the name of the Father . . . ." We both made the sign of the cross.

Then he folded his hands, leaned his elbows against his knees, and looked toward the ground.

"Bless me, Father, for I have sinned." I repeated the words my mom had taught me, before my very first confession. "My last confession was . . ." I thought back, "about six weeks ago. And I confess that, since that time, I've been disrespectful to my parents on a few different occasions." The priest nodded as I continued.

"I was listening to some music with really derogatory lyrics. I know that's not really helpful for the way I think about myself or others." More silence. My heart pounded as I thought of sitting next to Matt that morning in Mass.

"Okay, could you clarify something about this last one? Maybe you'll know whether it's really a sin." The priest looked up from the grass for a moment.

I recounted the story of resting my leg against this cute boy's, *Matt's,* leg. Then I pointed to the line in the examination of conscience. "Was that, 'purposefully touching another to sexually arouse?'" The priest smiled kindheartedly, and then asked, "Why do you think you were doing that?"

Why? Because it felt good. And because I wanted Matt to feel the same way about me. "I guess it was about controlling those feelings between us. I act like that around boys, a lot." I recognized a similar pattern in interactions with other guys. *I can change the outcome of a situation by either smiling at a cute boy or ignoring him. Or by tossing my hair, or laughing in a certain way, or placing my hand on his arm just long enough.* I had learned how to manipulate the force of sexual attraction.

The priest sat up straight, and remarked, "Christ commands us to love one another, as He loves us. That's what He's asking of you. Not to try to control or dominate anyone, but only to love."

I reflected quietly for a few minutes. *I care about Matt! Was I being loving toward him in Mass this morning?* The truth reflected back at me like a mirror.

No. I was playing The Game. It was the same game that those boys in summer camp played with me, when my limbs froze at their touch. *The same game that boy was playing when he called out at me earlier. I've been the target of this game before. How have my actions been much different than those guys'?*

After processing the priest's words, I confessed, "That wasn't loving, what I did."

The priest responded. "Let's praise God for the grace of a good confession. I suggest you pray for the gifts of modesty, chastity, and selflessness. I think that will really help. For your penance, I'll ask you to pray one Hail Mary for each of those virtues. Can you do that?"

I nodded, a frown gathering at my forehead. "Then please, say your Act of Contrition," he instructed, bowing his head again.

Internally, I wrestled with the meaning of the prayer I knew by heart, as I recited aloud:

"O my God, I am heartily sorry for having offended Thee," *I don't want to hurt You, Lord, by hurting any of your children.*

"And I detest all my sins because of Thy just punishments." *My parents said we're punished by the things in which we sin. Purposely toying with someone else's feelings, automatically makes me a player in the game I despise.*

"But most of all because they offend Thee, my God, Who art all-good and deserving of all my love." *How in the world am I going to change?*

"I firmly resolve, with the help of Thy grace . . ." *I'm promising here, but I'm going to need help!*

". . . to sin no more." *Please help me, Lord.*

"And to avoid the near occasion of sin." *Lead me not into temptation.*

"Amen."

The priest raised his arms in my direction and prayed the words of absolution:

"God, the Father of mercies, through the death and resurrection of his Son has reconciled the world to himself and sent the Holy Spirit among us for the forgiveness of sins. Through the ministry of the Church may God give you pardon and peace, and I absolve you from your sins in the name of the Father, and of the Son . . ." The priest motioned with his hand through the air. Following his lead, I crossed myself again.

". . . and of the Holy Spirit."

"Amen." I answered.

As I exited the tent, an overwhelming sense of impossibility descended upon me. I found a tree and sat in the abundant shade of its branches, leaning against its trunk. *I want to love like you love, Jesus. I don't want this double life, acting happy on the outside, but feeling disappointed and insecure on the inside. Help me treat others the way I want to be treated.* I thought of Matt's smiling face. *The way Matt treats me.*

A lot needs to change, in my heart and in my actions. The sturdy tree trunk stood as an image of God's stability against the whipping winds of apprehension. *I don't know how, but I trust You'll help me.* For starters, I decided to say my penance, every day. *One Hail Mary each, for modesty, chastity, and self-lessness. I can do that much.*

THE HILLTOP

June 21, 2003
After dark

Late that night, before heading to our dorms, Deacon Ken and Mrs. Buehler gathered the St. Francis and OLC youth groups together at the top of a grassy hill, near the fieldhouse. We had all been part of an emotional adoration session that night. "While we wait for a few more students to join us from confession," Deacon Ken addressed the group of us huddling on the darkened hilltop, "please take a few minutes to reflect on how God has worked in your heart this weekend."

I ran my fingers over blades of grass and prayed in my heart. *Adoration was beautiful but painful tonight, Lord. I meant it when I said that I'm tired of living a double life. The peace I have when I think about You is so real and inspiring, even though the challenge ahead seems insurmountable.*

Mrs. Buehler interrupted the silence. "Just a reminder that tomorrow morning, we'll have Mass and a closing session together, followed by our drive back home. We're going to stay in separate buses as we did on the drive down: Grand Rapids students in one motor coach, Rockford students in the other." *Maybe that'll be good. At least I'll give Matt more space.*

Deacon Ken added, "Would anyone like to share how this weekend might impact you once you return home?" A few people raised their hands. Deacon Ken called on someone. Heartfelt sharing commenced.

My prayer continued as the group discussion faded into gentle background noise. *I really desire to use my gifts for Your glory, instead of trying to glorify myself. Maybe those gifts include my body. Using my appearance to run the show hasn't made me happy anyway.*

Just then Matt quietly slid around the corner of the group. *He must've just finished in confession.* He sprawled out on the grass directly beside me, extended his arms wide, then clasped his hands behind his neck. Leaning back next to my waist, his elbow stretched across my lap. My pulse throbbed with the attraction that naturally ebbed between us. Keeping my sights on the starry night sky, I could sense him taking in my features. *I really don't think he's gay.*

Instinct dictated I should brush the soft hair away from his freckled forehead, stare back into his gray eyes, and forgo the entire inner struggle that was raging. *Help me, Lord.* A few fireflies twinkled around the field. And then another tug, deeper this time, pulled at my heart. *What is that?* It wasn't as sharp at my initial reaction, but it was distinctly stronger.

More than anything, I want what's best for Matt. Maybe that won't mean dating each other this summer. Maybe it won't even mean dating him at all during high school. I swallowed hard, attempting to ease the sadness tightening in my throat. *You opened incredible doors for my music when I waited for your lead, Lord. Will you guide me with Matt too? If you want this to happen, please open the door. I won't push it open myself. Amen*

Matt relaxed his arms and sat up in the grass beside me.

Chapter 4

BIG TENT AND BARE TRUTH
MATT

Anna's House
Sunday, March 15, 2009
9:10 A.M.

"ANNA'S HOUSE," the top of the menu read in bold letters. *I might as well figure out what I want before she gets here.*

Below, a list of typical midwestern breakfast dishes followed. As I perused through the omelettes, pancakes, and waffles, I thought of Amanda at fifteen. *She was always so sure of herself, even back then. It seemed like she knew exactly what she wanted, and she wasn't afraid to go after it.*

My relationship with my own wants, on the other hand, was always strained. As the fourth of five kids in my family, I never got to do what I wanted to do. Whether it was riding shotgun, the front passenger seat of the car, or "first bar" (the kitchen counter barstool on the end), there was always an older sibling arriving there first. And it was never my timeframe that took precedence. Someone else was always in more of a rush. But not getting what I wanted wasn't an altogether bad thing.

The result was that I was usually content. When you don't spend much time even acknowledging, much less fighting for, your own wants, it leaves a lot of space to enjoy the reality of how things naturally transpire. Often, that opened me to great new experiences that I wouldn't have even thought of! *Kind of like this breakfast.*

I wouldn't have invited Amanda to meet this morning. It certainly made me happy that she reached out, though. I wasn't sure what she might have to tell me, but knowing her, it would be something thoughtful and important. Even if she just wanted to meet for a quick talk, it would be great to spend time with her.

When we were fifteen, spending more time with her was one of my primary objectives. But I don't get what I want.

IS HE YOUR BOYFRIEND?

Steubenville, Ohio
June 21, 2003
Midmorning

The following summer, we were back in Steubenville again. This time, we had seen each other just once during the year at another retreat in Grand Rapids. We were both fifteen, so neither of us could drive yet. The distance between our lives had still appeared monumental during the school year. Convincing my parents to drive me twenty minutes into downtown Grand Rapids seemed far more daunting than the regular three-hour drive up north. Asking my family to change what we always did, just so I could go see a girl?! *No way.*

After starting the day with Mass, Amanda and I walked around campus during the morning break time. Our conversation and laughter easily kept us stepping in pace with each other. My sixteenth birthday was the following week, and with it came the anticipation of a driver's license and my own car. The chasm that opened wide between us when not on retreat seemed to be closing swiftly.

I didn't know how to explain that I was feeling closer to her, and I sure as heck didn't think Amanda would want me to mention it. So instead I talked about the conference. "It's so great to be back here!"

"Totally," Amanda agreed. She seemed to mirror my excitement. "Which do you prefer, these big regional conferences, or the fall retreat in Grand Rapids?"

"Oh, I like them both! You know what was sweet too? Your concert at the fall retreat." I remembered the joy and passion with which she played, how each word, each note, each prayer seemed to burst forth from her heart. "You even got us to stop playing football when we heard you outside." *How could anyone not want to listen to her sing and play?*

"Well, thanks." Amanda flashed all of her big pearly whites as she smiled wide. "That was so memorable."

She gestured excitedly with her hands as she described singing, playing piano, and sharing her faith. *She really sees performing her music as God's work. That must be why she has so much confidence and joy.*

She continued to describe what it was like sharing the music she wrote. *She's fearless! She doesn't seem to care at all what people might think about her. Sharing something that personal, and to so many people!*

"That sounds really awesome. Scary, but awesome. Do you think you'll do music for a career?" I asked. Our conversation continued to flow easily until a question barked out at us.

A big upperclassman aggressively shouted, "Hey! Girl! Is he your boyfriend, or what?" *Wait, is he seriously catcalling her? I've seen this happen in movies. Do people really do this?*

"Hey! Well . . ." Amanda said before I could gather myself.

Wait, he is serious. Amanda seems way less nervous about this than me. Man, she's cool under pressure, although maybe this isn't pressure for her. Does this kind of thing happen a lot to her?

Why's everyone looking at me? Are they expecting me to know what to say?

"No!" I blurted out, emphatically stating the truth. I shook my head back and forth quickly. "No, no . . ." *And since I'm not, I don't want anybody to think I think I am. If Amanda knew that's what I wanted she would definitely stop talking to me.* ". . . no." *Why's he putting me on the spot like this?*

"If this clown's not your boyfriend, then who is?" *He's not letting up.*

"I don't have a boyfriend. Thanks for asking, but we're gonna keep walking now," came Amanda's surprisingly calm response.

"When you change your mind, how will I know? Unless I get your number?" *Wow, that's bold. Does that work?*

"I don't give my number to guys I've just met." *Oh, I guess not.* But she did smile at him. *Does she like that kind of boldness?*

Amanda explained that we had to get going, and with a firm push on my shoulder she spun around, starting off in the opposite direction. I followed suit and happily strode away from the confrontational upperclassman.

I'm glad that's over.

"You know, you could just say 'yes,'" Amanda stated evenly.

"What do you mean?" *Yes, what?*

She sped up, but turned to look one last time at him. "If some guy's harassing me. You could just say you're my boyfriend."

"Oh!" *Wait, really? She wants me to say I'm her boyfriend? As if that could ever happen.* She was cooler than me, clearly prettier than me, and more mature. *She's way out of my league. Why **would** she want me to say that? I suppose if it helped her brush off some other guy.*

"Okay! Yeah, next time." Insecurity swirled as my thoughts turned further inward. *How will I know if she's being harassed? What if I say it and she's not? That would be super awkward.*

THE PORTIUNCULA

June 21, 2003
Afternoon

On the edge of the Franciscan campus, nestled against the forest, was a small chapel of stone and wood. A glossy pamphlet near the door described the history of the Portiuncula: a replica of the quiet haven where St. Francis of Assisi and his early friars made their community home in the 1300s.

It was a peaceful space, the kind that instantly lifted your mind to God. *Perfect. Thank you, Lord, for this place!* I walked in and knelt about halfway in on the right. There were fewer people there.

My Lord and my God! I come before You here to rest in your presence. Thank You, my Savior, thank You. I trust in Your love. O Lord, why is it so much easier here? Why do I keep messing up when I know Your way is better?

A searing stab of shame and guilt cut through me. *I'm so weak.* A rapid flash of images rolled through my head. I squeezed my eyes against them and shook my head. *Forgive me, Lord! Why do I look at them? Why search them out?*

It had been less than a year since I had stumbled upon some of the darkness to be found on the internet. A few guys at school bragged about their exploits online. *How could they be proud of that?* I was just left feeling hollow. And yet, there was something about those images that drew me back.

I know I shouldn't search after them, Lord, but I can't seem to help it. Even when I'm surfing something else, I could feel the pull toward more and more risqué sites. There was something alluring about the search. But without fail, it had left me feeling worse than when I started. *I know that doesn't glorify You. Help me, Lord!*

How can I sing and praise and pray with such joy on retreat, while the darkness gathers at the edge, waiting to pull me back in? I don't want that, Lord. I want You.

Seek My forgiveness

Confession—I need to take this to confession. It's gonna be really embarrassing telling this to a priest!

Seek My forgiveness

I'll go. Give me the strength to be honest.

I knew there was confession happening. There would also be priests available later in the evening, though. *I'll go then. That'll give me more time to prepare.* I decided to find Amanda instead, for the time being. *Life is always brighter when her laugh's ringing in the air.*

THE HILLTOP

June 21, 2003
After dark

I sat down next to the priest, thankful that the order of confession was on the blue construction paper in my hand, yet I still felt unable to begin. *Do I say something first, or does he?* I couldn't get a read off of the priest since my eyes were glued to the floor. *It's hard enough to even look up. How am I going to explain that I haven't been to confession in almost a year?*

"Let's begin in the name of the Father, and of the Son, and of the Holy Spirit," the priest said.

I followed along with the familiar beginning.

"How long has it been since your last confession?"

My eyes bore deeper into the floor. Memories of the fall retreat in Grand Rapids bubbled up. "Not quite a year."

"Jesus rejoices and welcomes you back to this sacrament of mercy. What have you come to confess today?"

"Well," my voice caught. *Come on, you prepared for this.* Looking at the now crumpled blue paper kickstarted the litany I had prepared. "I've been judgmental. I've been mean. I've used my humor to hurt people, not just to make them laugh. I've lied to my parents and my friends, mostly to get out of trouble or to make myself look better." A few more of my well-rehearsed sins tumbled out as I released them into the air around us. There was one last topic to broach. My mouth opened, but no words came out. My head sunk lower, well past my slumped shoulders now. I tried again. It caught once more in my throat.

Breaking the silence, the priest gently offered, "If there's something you don't want to say, that's probably what the Lord desires for you to say most."

A cycle of emotions started up again within me. It was a cycle that had been swirling since that morning in the Portiuncula. I had spent an entire afternoon psyching myself up for this, after the time in adoration had crystallized what I needed to bring up. But bringing it to light in prayer had increased the weight of guilt even as I sang and prayed.

Embarrassment. *I don't want anyone to know what I've done!*
Shame. *I know better. I shouldn't have fallen so low.*
Dread. *What is the priest going to say to me?*
Honesty. *I know what I am doing is hurting me.*
Sorrow. *And I know that it hurts God!*
Contrition. *I don't want to do this anymore!*

Resolve. *I need help.*

I just need to say it.

"I've also been giving in to lust—with pornography and masturbation."

Relief. As those words were pushed out, they drew with them the weight of guilt, self-judgment, and pride. I inhaled sharply and straightened up a bit. "For these and all my sins, I am truly sorry." *Forgive me, Lord! I want to be better!* The priest began speaking with gentle words about God's love and mercy and about God's desire for us to walk in the light. With each encouragement, I sat up a little straighter. With each breath, another layer of weighted shame fell off. Finally I looked up at the priest.

He prescribed a simple penance: to pray the Our Father slowly, really thinking about each word. At his prompting, I read the Act of Contrition off the now *very* crumpled blue paper. Then raising his hand over my head, the priest prayed the words of absolution and set me free.

As I walked away from the chapel, my heart soared so free and so light that my feet hardly bent the grass. *All right! Thank You, Lord!* A breathy laugh escaped through my open grin. *Thank You! A clean slate. A fresh start. Another chance.*

The heaviness that had been pressing on my heart since adoration in the Portiuncula that afternoon was completely lifted. The grime and gunk that had been building up in my soul, which I had started seeking, was washed away. *Thank You, Lord!* I had just discovered a new dimension of God's love in my life—the freedom of admitting fault and seeking forgiveness.

I ran up the hill to where our group was meeting and let out another laugh. *What a beautiful evening!* The fullness of God's love, through the sacrament of Confession, surrounded me. I could see it everywhere I looked.

My eyes fell on Amanda sitting at the edge of the group with ample open grass right next to her. *I gotta tell her how great I feel! I don't know if I would have been ready to go to confession tonight without seeing her joy and amazing faith.* The grin I had been holding since the priest's words of absolution widened.

Maybe it's time to be a bit more bold.

I know I like Amanda. I smile when I see her. I'm filled with joy when she laughs. I'm happy when she is happy. I want to keep making her happy.

Without the burden of my guilt pressing down on me, and with a new understanding of God's love, I could accomplish anything.

Well, if I actually was her boyfriend, that'd give us a lot more time together.

With my heart in the clouds, I sprang over to her and flopped down with my head near the grass she had been absently pulling. Someone else in the group was sharing about their day so Amanda withheld a greeting.

Resting my hands under my head, my bent arm settled across her lap. *My goodness, she is beautiful.*

She kept looking out at the sky. *Was this too forward? She knows this means I like her, right? What if she thinks that's stupid? No, she's way better than that. The way she's able to pray and sing in front of all of those people, she won't make fun of me for being honest.* I relaxed a bit more into her.

I want to know this joy always. The joy of forgiveness, purity, and love. I want Your joy, Lord. As the next person started sharing, Amanda still hadn't moved much. *I thought she'd at least play with my hair.* In truth, it wasn't that comfortable a position, so I sat up, nudging her with my shoulder.

She gave me a light smile, nothing more. The hopes that had just blossomed before me suddenly seemed foolish. *She doesn't like me like that.* And yet that was okay. *Being even this close to her is enough.* Peace and freedom were still reverberating in my soul. *If just being her friend on these retreats is what will make her the happiest, then I'm happy with that too.*

How I'd Like to Be

Verse 1

A graceful, blessed, virgin woman
She knows just who she is
Not afraid of speaking up
She asks the right questions
And when she's called to give her best
Has no problem saying yes

Chorus

She is the light for me
She is how I'd like to be
Looking to her, I find Thee
Finding You I find out my identity
She is how I'd like to be

Verse 2

A wife, a mother, a cousin, a friend
She's always quick to serve
She knows how to take a compliment
Gives credit when it's deserved
Traveling, shedding doubt
Fitting in, standing out

Bridge

In your darkest hour
She never leaves your side
She need not say a word
She says it with her eyes
And when she speaks
News of peace
I fall down to my knees

A DIFFERENT DIRECTION
AMANDA

Anna's House
Sunday, March 15, 2009
9:11 A.M.

Powder from the salt trucks still coated the pavement as I stepped out of my car into the parking lot of Anna's House. The air was cold enough to make breathing visible. "Bless the Lord," was the word on my lips.

Before leaving the house that morning, I had asked my younger brother to join me for the Liturgy of the Hours, also known as the Divine Office. Said at specific times through the day, at each and every hour of every day, somewhere around the world Catholics are praying the same psalms and Scripture passages. There was something comforting about the universality of it. "What stood out to you from the readings?" I asked my brother at the end of prayer.

"Bless the Lord! They kept saying it," he replied.

Filtering through layers of wispy clouds, the sun attempted to coax some sparkle out of the gray snowbanks scattered throughout the parking lot. *Cold and chill, bless the Lord!* I briefly surveyed my reflection, mirrored in the glass entryway of the restaurant.

The front of my hair was secured with a few hidden bobby pins, leaving several loose ringlets to frame my face. The rest of my dark tresses fell in waves down my back. A deep-green turtleneck sweater fit snugly underneath a crisp, white, winter vest, and brown suede boots were laced tightly around slate-colored skinny jeans.

Servants of the Lord, bless the Lord. Praise and exalt him above all forever.

Laying one hand on the metal door handle, I reclaimed the interior freedom I gained as my feelings for Matt deepened as a teenager.

Freedom to be okay with myself: heart, mind, and body.
  Bless the Lord.
Freedom to stop grasping for validation from guys.
  Bless the Lord.
Freedom to look out for others, instead of only for myself.
  Bless the Lord.
Freedom to love, as Christ loves me.
  Bless the Lord.

THE SPOT FOR ME

Grand Rapids, Michigan
February 24, 2004
Evening

Several months after the iconic confession under the big white tent in Steubenville, our St. Francis youth group gathered for a Mardi Gras party. It was one of those nights when we got together just for the fun of it, to play in the snow and eat snacks together. We were at the home of the Ramirez family, who opened their sledding hill and their basement for the maybe twenty students who showed up. At age sixteen, the majority of my friendships were still from youth group.

"I can't feel my nose," Kevin said, sniffing.

"A couple hours of sledding will do that for you, Kev," I said, shaking my hair out. Small bits of snow fell around my feet, still numb from the cold despite two thick pairs of socks. "Lent starts tomorrow. Better fill up while we still can," I reminded him.

After tossing my hat onto the mound of boots, gloves, and coats by the door, I surveyed the snack table. With a plateful of brownies in one hand and a plastic cup of soda pop in the other, it was time to investigate where the cool kids were hanging out. Halfway down the basement staircase, the card table in the back left of the room came into sight. *There's one empty chair in the corner.* On either side of it sat Bobby and Tino, two of the nicest (and nicest-looking) guys at the party.

Before taking the next step, I envisioned the upcoming scene. *It'll be a small space to slide into. Our arms will be brushing, our legs bumping against each others'.* In an instant, I remembered the line from that convicting examination of conscience the summer before. "Have you purposely exchanged words, glances, or touches with another or with yourself to sexually arouse?" *Lord, help me!*

Then, over to the right, I saw Brittany.

She sat alone. I knew what I needed to do. I took a deep breath, and my feet headed down the rest of the staircase in her direction.

"Hey Brittany, may I sit next to you?"

"Sure," she said with a friendly shrug.

"So, sledding. Pretty fun, huh?"

"Really fun! Especially the huge jump."

A few other kids came over to sit next to us, armed with a month's supply of goodies. The first bite of brownie signaled culinary success. "Oh, these are delicious! Gooey, but not too gooey. And the frosting is so rich. This is what Fat Tuesday is supposed to taste like," I said, thoroughly enjoying the dessert after hours of sledding.

"My mom made those brownies!" Brittany boasted. By the end of the night, everyone had a chance to laugh together. I even spent time talking with Bobby and Tino before returning home.

The following day, another friend, Katie, signed on to AIM.

KatieBugg11: so did you have a good time at the party?

EbonyAndIvory: definitely! did you?

KatieBugg11: yeah I did :)

KatieBugg11: but my sister Brittany said she was feeling really sad and really left out, until you came to sit by her. and then she said she had a great time.

I leaned back from the computer screen.

I had no idea what that would mean to Brittany.

The many Hail Marys prayed for the virtues of modesty, chastity, and selflessness came to mind. *Maybe it wasn't a coincidence. Maybe the Holy Spirit was working in me. Loving through me.*

If the command of the Holy Spirit meant serving others in need, then I wanted to keep following.

Recalling the big hug that Bobby gave me before I left the sledding party, I continued to ponder. *Maybe loving means being open to the gifts God wants to give me, instead of grasping for them myself.* Waiting to talk to the nice, cute guys seemed like a small price to pay for helping someone else to feel loved.

CEDAR SPRINGS

Rockford, Michigan
March 26, 2004
Dusk

That same Lent, Mrs. Buehler called with an invitation to lead music for another high-school retreat, for Our Lady of Consolation. I had moved from being a volunteer teen leader to being paid to lead music ministry. *Getting hired to sing?! Sweet!* Matt and I hadn't chatted online often during the school year, so I wasn't sure whether he'd show up. *Will he be there too? And will we still get along?*

I still thought of Matt and prayed for him each day. Together with the daily prayers for modesty, chastity, and selflessness, my actions had followed suit. My radio no longer blasted objectifying lyrics. Flirtatious online chatting halted. Gossip about "hot guys" dwindled. Some of my closest friends and I didn't have much to talk about anymore.

Dusk was cold and dreary as the students gathered in Rockford. Along with about twenty other high-school teens, Matt was there! *He seems more shy this time. Or maybe it's just that I've grown more confident.*

"Choose one of the vans. We'll have a brief drive up to Cedar Springs," Mrs. Buehler instructed the group. *I want to sit by Matt.* With a sigh, I realized the seating would be crowded. Matt hopped up into one van. I chose the other.

Country music. Corny jokes. The smell of musty tennis shoes. *I could be snuggling next to Matt right now.* Although my actions were changing, my heart was taking longer to catch up. When the vans finally arrived at the retreat center, we checked into one of the small wooden cabins among rows of tall cedar trees.

The first evening of the retreat had been less than enchanting. Cheesy skits, meager participation in the singing, keeping a reasonable distance from Matt, although I preferred to stay beside him. *My feelings have somehow strengthened since the summer.* The highlight of the night was watching Matt make everyone around him laugh.

A great conflict raged between my head and my heart. On the one hand, I knew it would be wrong to purposely stir up sexual tension with Matt. On the other hand, I really wanted to be more than just friends! I didn't know how to move that process along without manipulating the chemistry between us.

For the first half of the retreat, I vacillated between giving Matt so much space that I wasn't even in his line of vision and dropping colossal hints at my openness to dating him. He didn't pick up on any of my relationship cues, however, not even the most obvious one at lunch on the second day of retreat.

"Hey, Amanda?" Matt asked at the table.

"Matt, *whatever* your question is, the answer is 'yes.'" I stared him squarely in the face, a twinkle in my eye.

"Ah . . . would you pass the orange juice?"

Finally, during downtime that afternoon, Matt asked if I wanted to take a walk with him. We were exploring the forest together, just the two of us. Far away from the city, no traffic could be heard. Dried pine needles crunched underfoot.

"These trees are beautiful." *They're serene, graceful, standing tall, stretching to the heights. Not stooping to hide their grandeur, nor straining to prove their worth. That's how I'd like to be.*

"Mmm hmm," Matt agreed, looking up.

"I wonder how they're able to cut all the branches so the pine needles will only grow at the top," I said.

"No one cuts them," Matt clarified, pointing to the tree trunks. "They're planted so close together, that the sun only reaches the treetops. Branches can only grow when they're exposed to direct sunlight."

"Oh, wow!" I laughed, comparing this new information with my mental image of lumberjacks routinely shaving the sides of the tree trunks. *It's cool how Matt knows about all these country things.* I deeply desired to disclose my feelings for him and to ask Matt to tell me about his.

Should I tell him? For some reason, I lost a sense of peace deep inside my soul at the thought of initiating that conversation.

Maybe if I just chill and let him lead, that would work better.

Matt changed the subject to our recent foosball match. We walked and joked awhile longer. I tried to maintain my composure. As we arrived back at the lodge, I said, "Well, I'm gonna go brush my teeth before leading the next round of music." *Brush my teeth? Really cool, Amanda.*

RELATIONSHIP GOALS

Rockford, Michigan
March 28, 2004
Late morning

For Mass on the final day of the Cedar Springs retreat, we returned to Rockford. In the open, contemporary OLC church building, the retreatants took up two of the padded pews, surrounded by a large congregation of kids, parents, and grandparents. Even as I cherished the final moments with Matt, dreams of the future developed in my imagination.

After Matt graduates high school, we could start an actual dating relationship. And then, after a few years, we could get engaged. Matt could be a real estate agent, like his dad. Maybe Matt could become a deacon too. Eventually, I'd get a job as a music director for a church, after we start our family. Ten kids sounds like a good amount.

"This Lenten season, the Church invites us into the desert with Jesus," proclaimed the pastor, Fr. Tom. Rather than listening attentively, as my demeanor might have depicted, I allowed my thoughts to wander all the more. His preaching became a colorful backdrop to my musings.

Sitting next to Matt during the homily was enough of an exercise in self-control. *Every time I shift at all, he does too.* I extended my legs. So did Matt. After a few moments, I tucked my legs back under my chair. Matt did the same. *I read about this in a magazine article!* They called it "mirroring body language."

Fr. Tom continued preaching, picking up steam.

I ran through the mental list of reasons Matt and I would be perfect together:

> *Makes me laugh*
> *Laughs at my jokes*
> *Really listens*
> *Prays*
> *Probably is rich . . .*

My mom had informed me that Matt's dad was not only a real estate agent himself but also the owner of a large company of many real estate agents. Matt was more than materially wealthy, though. *He also has a big, loving, faith-filled family.*

> *. . . Gets along with his brothers and sisters*
> *Is kind to people who are weaker than he is*
> *Is so cute*
> *Loves to play*
> *Understands nature-y things*

The tone of the preaching intensified, the words emphatic. My emotions swelled.

Most of all, though, Matt's not like the guys who only care about my body, or like the girls who just focus on popularity. The homily was clearly reaching its pinnacle.

Besides doing music, I've never wanted anything so badly.

I stretched my legs again. Matt mirrored. *We have a couple years of high school left, though. What can I do about these feelings now? That is, if I'm serious about the whole chastity thing?*

Matt was absently edging his foot toward mine. I slid my legs back again and thought of adoration the night before: teens crying with joy, stories of healing and renewal. *How does that happen every time?*

In the background, Fr. Tom's voice softened.

Maybe this weekend was meant to teach me something. There wasn't much to work with on retreat: a small wood cabin, silly skits, songs with timid singers, and some simple prayers. But Jesus was there! So miracles happened. A comforting sensation of warmth kindled in my chest. Goosebumps dotted my arms, inside the long-sleeved cotton shirt from the retreat.

There's also not a lot to work with between Matt and me. We hardly ever see each other. When we do, we don't talk about anything complex. These little sacrifices I'm making, they're not much! It's all pretty simple. Matt was looking toward the front of church, listening to the homily. *But Jesus must be here between us.*

The preaching seemed to be winding down, in any case.

With zero physical payoff, Matt still seems to like me so much! I'm never happier than when we're together. The more Matt has been in my life, the more my other relationships have become about God. Plus, I'm praying, every day, when I think of him. Matt's leading me to Jesus.

So when should we get married? I laughed at myself under my breath.

Fr. Tom gave an exaggerated nod to finish the sermon and resumed his seat in the presider's chair.

Jesus, I prayed in the quiet. *Following You like this is an answer to prayer. I'm not using Matt! I'm thinking of what's best for him. I'm trying to be patient! But there's gotta be more, right?* A song from the retreat resounded in my heart: "All of you is more than enough for all of me."

I surrender this too, Jesus. Whenever I trust in You, there's always more.

That day marked a few significant decisions. I wasn't going to keep asking Matt about getting together anymore. I also wasn't going to initiate any sort of dating relationship. As soon as we were both finished with high school, though, I would definitely let Matt know how I felt about him.

For the next few years, I didn't give anyone else a second thought.

Granted, there were plenty of attractive guys around. Dating someone besides Matt, though, was never appealing (even when David Shaheen—my Confirmation Crush—finally showed interest in me during my senior year of high school). I counted down the days until Matt would graduate, and I hoped with all my heart that he was waiting for me too.

Chapter 5

A DIFFERENT DIRECTION
MATT

Anna's House
Sunday, March 15, 2009
9:12 A.M.

Is that her car? According to her last text, she should be arriving about now. I felt a small hit of adrenaline as my heartbeat quickened and my sweat glands threatened action. *Is it her?* A large white woman got out of the driver's side and three kids spilled out of the other. *Nope, not yet.*

By now, I was feeling annoyed. Not at Amanda's tardiness, but at my own eagerness. *There's nothing to be nervous about. It will be as easy as it ever was talking with her again.*

I turned to the waitress as she refilled my coffee for the second time. *I suppose this isn't helping my nerves.*

My eyes snapped back to their post guarding the parking lot in time to see her step out of a bronze sedan. Dark hair fell thick around her shoulders. Her bright white vest and tall boots seemed more fashionable than practical, but I wasn't going to complain. *Goodness.*

Bless the Lord, all you works of the Lord! The line from my morning prayer rang out again. *Thank You for the beauty You have created, Lord! Give me the strength to praise You for it.*

I knew all too well that I didn't always have that strength. There were times when seeing the beauty of God's creation lifted my heart to immediate prayer and praise. Yet I also sometimes got tripped up by that same beauty. Those same old shadows from my teen years were still clinging to me at twenty-one, try as I might to shake them off completely.

May the beauty of Your creation help me glorify You, Lord.

She disappeared from sight as she walked up to the door.

Fire and heat, bless the Lord.

Cold and chill, bless the Lord.

Recalling more of the Scripture, I set my soul at ease again.

Spirits and souls of the just, bless the Lord.

Holy men of humble heart, bless the Lord.

I ran my hand through my hair in a last-ditch attempt to straighten it out. I felt the cowlick sticking up in back. *I shoulda gotten a haircut. Too late now. Perfect hair never mattered when we were kids, after all.* Nearly all of our previous interactions had been on overnight retreats, where appearances mattered far less than recognizing God in our midst.

CEDAR SPRINGS

Cedar Springs, Michigan
March 27, 2004
After dark

"All of You is more than enough for all of me, for every thirst and every need." Eyes closed, kneeling tall, hands raised open before me, my heart filled to bursting, I sang along with

Amanda. "You satisfy me with Your love, and all I have in You is more than enough."

She was again leading us in song during adoration. With her keyboard, amazing voice, and deep faith, she helped draw all of us high schoolers into this moment of encounter with Jesus. Our Savior was present here among us in the Eucharist. Amanda helped us feel it. *Thank You, Lord, for the beauty of nature around us. And thank You for Your beauty so clearly seen in Amanda.*

This retreat was similar to those summer conferences, except with the benefit of being close to home. The simple building, nestled in the woods, provided a peaceful, reflective tone. The setting made it easy to muse on the beauty of God's creation. Spending time with Amanda also made that easy.

Amanda was, without a doubt, the most beautiful girl I knew. *And she talks to me!* Everything about her was attractive to me. Her thick dark hair, smooth dark skin. That beauty mark just above her lip was captivating. *And she was nice!* At age sixteen, it seemed that most of the other girls I knew got meaner the prettier they were. Not so for Amanda. Her joy and enthusiasm rang out freely for everyone.

Help me see everything beautiful as a gift of Your creation. There's nothing else I want, Lord. Thank You for this moment. You are all I need. In the midst of so confident a prayer, a darker thought cut in. *What about the joy you find looking at porn?*

I leaned back, to sit against my feet. My hands dropped to my sides. *Forgive me, Lord.* A series of lewd images flashed before me. I banished the thoughts, but the shame lingered on. *I'm sorry, Lord! I don't want to be tied by them!*

I knew that those sites I found online and returned to when the house was quiet were hurting me. I knew they were drawing me away from God. *I know it's sinful. And yet. There's such a pull.* It felt like gravity or the tides: a force that couldn't be fought. *The thrill is so fleeting, though! And it always leaves me feeling worse.*

Here in Your love, Lord, this is real, this is what lasts. I choose this. I want to choose you always! Give me the strength to choose you.

"More than all I want, more than all I need, You are more than enough for me! More than all I know, more than all I see, You are more than enough!" Amanda sang out boldly the words that were forming in my heart. *I want more of You, God! I want only You! Only You really fill the emptiness, only You leave me feeling whole.*

A peace settled into my heart. I lifted myself back up on my knees. A full grin spread across a face that had just been shedding tears of anguish. I raised my hands again as I stared into the monstrance. Mercy and hope swirled about me as a new song began.

I can do this, Lord. Help me to live for You always!

REFLECTING

Rockford, Michigan
Friday, February 4, 2005
After midnight

"Slow down! Proceed with caution!" the yellow traffic lights seemed to shout out into the dark night as they flashed. *Too late for that. Where were you an hour ago?* But no, there had been warning signs. I just ignored them.

I knew the route well. It was just about four miles between my girlfriend's house and mine. The fact that the traffic lights had switched from their normal cycle to blinking yellow indicated I had again stayed out too late.

The outside lights were on, but the rest of the house looked dark. I parked at the far end of the driveway and walked, head down, to the door. The stars shone bright and clear, but I didn't notice. I got inside, turned off the outside lights, and headed upstairs.

Hands planted firmly on the bathroom countertop, I stared back at myself. *Why?! Come on, Matt, you're better than that!* This mirror soul-searching was becoming a common practice. After dating for half a year, we had started to get very comfortable. *Too comfortable. I thought we were stronger than that.* She wasn't Catholic, but was very active and committed to the Baptist church her family attended. *I thought Baptists were supposed to be even more uptight about this stuff. But no, it's certainly not all on her.*

We had talked early on in our relationship about how chastity was an important virtue of our faith. There were certain physical things that we knew we had to wait to do. We were open about what some of our friends were doing and how that was "going too far." Then again, I did kiss her before we started dating. We had gotten very close since we were both in the fall play and our characters were dating. *That wasn't a healthy relationship either.* Orin Scrivello, the masochist dentist, and Audrey from *The Little Shop of Horrors. That was fun, though.*

That's the problem, I suppose. It's fun. We still held firm on certain boundaries. There were still some lines we didn't cross, even if we seemed to be running toward them. And those edges were moving, lines that stopped us before we now stepped over with barely a pause. *How much longer before all the lines get crossed?*

The look of self-loathing that stared back tonight was even harsher since I had gone into the night with a firm resolve about where I would draw the line. But firmness shifted lightning quick with just a few promptings from her.

You're too weak.

You are too weak alone, came the response.

Lord, I even prayed for strength tonight! What the heck!
    You are too weak alone.

The evening had been going well. We had laughed, talked, and played Scrabble. *She beat me again.* Thinking of that
happy look of triumph on her face made me smile in spite of
myself. *It was a perfect evening. Why did we even put a movie
on? We both knew exactly what would happen, lying on that
couch together.*

*I've got to do better. We've got to do better. Next time we can.
Help us, Lord.*

ASH WEDNESDAY

February 9, 2005
Late afternoon

"I want to give up something more than just chocolate for Lent
this year." *Perfect, she's bringing it up.* "I mean, I loooove chocolate, so it's a big sacrifice. But that's what I always do." Even
though she was Baptist, her family took Lent pretty seriously. "I
think I'm going to give up Starbucks. That is going to be really
hard!" *Oh, yeah. Starbucks.*

"What are you going to give up, Matty?"

"Well, uh, actually, I was, uh, thinking of something different," I stuttered, failing to keep my voice even.

"Oh yeah, harder than not coming to practice with a frap-
puccino?"

"Yeah, definitely." I took one more deep breath, and the
words rushed out. "I think we should give up all physical stuff
for Lent." She looked back, surprised. I continued. "Well, we
both know that we have been going too far lately, right?"

"Right," she replied weakly.

"I think it'll be good for us. Because we're doing way too much lately." She nodded but didn't seem convinced.

"Like no physical stuff at all? Not even a hug or kiss good night?"

She leaned in for a kiss. *Well, not everything.* I grinned as she got close, and I kissed her softly on the lips.

"No, we don't need to be Puritans for Lent. But I think we should talk about what we won't do."

Shortly, we settled on clear, definable boundaries that we would reestablish for Lent.

Thank You, Lord, for the courage to bring that up. And thank You for the faith to see how important it is. Help us to live up to it.

FRIDAY, SECOND WEEK OF LENT

February 18, 2005
After midnight

What the heck! screamed the look of disappointment staring deep into my eyes. *Two weeks, that's it!*

I looked away, back down at my hands, once more planted firmly on the bathroom countertop. I couldn't hold my own gaze any longer. I knew the mirror only held the shame and weakness of self-betrayal.

Two weeks into Lent and already we had failed. *We didn't even put up a fight today. We practically ran over those boundaries. So weak.*

Forgive me, Lord. I am so weak. I am sorry. Give me the strength to do better. Give me the strength to be better.

Please Come Back to Me

Verse 1

You'll never get this song
I'm writing at my piano, resigned to let it go
I'll keep my cool
You'll think that I'm nobody's fool
But every time I play these notes
My heart will know

Chorus

This is my
Please come back to me
Please come back to me
Please come back to me song
This is my
Please come back to me
Please come back to me
Please come back to me song

Verse 2

You'll never see
All you mean to me
I'll bottle it up
So it will always keep
I'll play it cool
You'll think that I'm nobody's fool
But every time I sing these notes
My heart will know

Bridge

Nobody wants to sound desperate
And I'm no exception
If you love somebody let 'em go
Well I let you go so long ago
And you're still gone
Except
And you're still gone
Except when I
And you're still gone
Except when I play this song

ANNA'S HOUSE
AMANDA

Anna's House
Sunday, March 15, 2009
9:12 A.M.

Here we go. Across the room, Matt stood to greet me. *It's always great to see him.* I weaved past a few empty tables, over the checkered linoleum. *Same easy smile, plus some facial hair.* A quick hug, and then he nodded toward the table. "It's good to see you—twice in one weekend!" he said cheerily.

"I'm glad you could make the drive up." I slid into the smooth leather booth and set my brown suede purse on the seat beside me. *And so it begins.* A few pairs of customers were seated around the restaurant, beneath hanging lamps. *How to bring up our past?*

"Well, thanks for inviting me. Notre Dame isn't too far," Matt observed with a smile. *Rockford was so far away for all those years, but now another state seems close. Perspective!*

We proceeded to talk about coffee, the music ministry event I had given the day before, and whether I might go running later. *We're talking. At a restaurant. Together. Like normal friends.* Matt even mentioned paying for the bill. *This is so far from normal, though.*

We silently scanned the menus for a few moments. I savored the irony of our first "date," willing myself not to laugh as I thought of the fateful conversation that had thrown my original relationship goals off course.

JOINING SEMINARY

Grand Rapids, Michigan
May 3, 2006
Evening

I had taken a year off school before starting college to work on my music. Still a senior in high school, Matt's screen name rarely appeared online anymore. Among our few mutual friends, Tony Oleck usually knew how Matt was doing. All of our parents knew each other, so Tony was a trusted source of information.

Tony's dad had sold my parents our house. The Olecks were devout Catholics, and Mr. Oleck just so happened to work in the agency that Mr. Fase, *Matt's dad,* owned. *It's a small Catholic world, after all.* Tony was close to my sister's age, but he always had the scoop on Matt.

Our conversation over AIM that spring rolled over my heart like ominous, black clouds on a formerly sunny day.

TonyOleck4Life: did you hear where Matt Fase is going to college?

Tell me, tell me, tell me! We've hardly talked since the Cedar Springs retreat two years ago.

EbonyandIvory: Where? Haven't heard from Matt in a while.

Aside from the time I saw him in passing, before one of my concerts. Why was he so distant then? "I'm just dropping Mary off," was about the only thing he said to me.

TonyOleck4Life: Holy Cross College. It's down in South Bend, Indiana, right next to Notre Dame.

I've sung in South Bend before. That's less than two hours away. A long-distance relationship would be fine with me.

TonyOleck4Life: The best part is that he was accepted into the Old College seminary program!

EbonyandIvory: Seminary?

But, Catholic seminaries lead to . . .

The priesthood.

Like, the never-getting-married-or-having-a-family kind of priesthood?!

Time stood still, as *"TonyOleck4life is typing,"* appeared in the text of our chat box. The pulsing force of anticipation coursed through my veins.

TonyOleck4life: To become a priest! Isn't that exciting?

I covered my face with my hands. The ticking of the wall clock taunted me. It counted down the seconds like I had counted down the months until Matt and I could start dating.

Matt's going to school out of state. To join the seminary. My heart leapt up into my throat for a second before sinking with the weight of reality. *After waiting and waiting to reconnect after high school! He's studying to become a priest.*

Maybe he'll discern out. That hopeful thought was the silver lining to an overcast future.

AS SEEN ON TV

Irondale, Alabama
January 17, 2007
After dark

During Matt's second semester in seminary, I was invited as a guest on an internationally broadcast talk show filmed in

Alabama. From my guesthouse at the studio, I composed an email for my friends and family, inviting them to tune in. *What about including Matt in this message too?*

I stared at the compose box of my laptop, thinking back on the past several months.

One rare occasion the previous summer, Matt's screen name appeared online. I congratulated him on his plans to join the seminary. He had responded with his new school email address and the adage, "Let's stay in touch!"

Each time I had considered contacting him again, something like an invisible force field interrupted my thoughts.

> *I could email him and—Boom!*
> *No, don't do it.*

This wasn't an audible voice so much as a distinct, interior sense.

> *Maybe if I just text him, we could—*
> *Do not go there.*

Lord. If that's You, I'm listening. I'll wait for Your timing. I won't distract Matt. He needs to base his discernment on You, not on me.

My heart sank a bit more with each day that went by without a word from Matt. I even attempted, multiple times, to write a song entitled "Move On." The writing process only produced a scowl and crumpled pieces of paper.

While Matt began his first semester, I tried seeing other guys. It never lasted past the second date. In short, they weren't him.

So I had thrown myself into music, networking ceaselessly and singing for anyone who would listen. I had already begun carving out a niche in youth-focused Catholic music. Concerts for churches and youth groups had led to opportunities to sing at diocesan events, and even national gatherings (like the National Black Catholic Congress). As I sold CDs at each concert, I would save up the money and then put it back into another new album. It wasn't quite full-time work yet, but together with a standing gig playing music at St. Francis, I was building toward a legitimate career as a music artist.

Looking at my list of email contacts in Irondale that night, I posed the question again, this time to God. *Should I include Matt?* A sense of calm surrounded the idea. Checking the box beside his school email address, I hit send.

The thrill of singing and speaking on live TV the next day was rivaled by the excitement of the automated email notification from my website afterward. "New member: Matt Fase."

KEEPING TABS

Grand Rapids, Michigan
May 23, 2007
Evening

Since appearing on live TV in January, a notification consistently showed up in the right-hand corner of my website: "Logged in: Matt Fase." *Is this a programming glitch? Is Matt really visiting my website every day?*

Seeing his name on my website was the most contact we had. Matt was never logged on to AIM anymore. I knew lots of college students had started to use Facebook instead, but I hadn't joined social media yet. *Perhaps if I just send him another email—Boom!* The invisible force would counter.

Although we never talked anymore, and I had taken his picture down from beside my bed, each nightfall brought thoughts of Matt as I drifted to sleep.

Since Tony Oleck was himself now considering joining religious life, he kept me abreast of Matt's progress in the seminary. With the sound of an opening door, Tony's screen name appeared online that spring.

TonyOleck4Life: Did you hear about Matt?

EbonyandIvory: Nope

TonyOleck4Life: He signed up for a second year!

For the first time, I wondered what my life would be like if Matt became a priest.

ANNA'S HOUSE
MATT

Anna's House
Sunday, March 15, 2009
9:12 A.M.

I stood up as Amanda came in and smiled at the hostess. Amanda strode over to where I was standing by our table. *Handshake, hug, high five?* As she got closer, her smile brightened and her arms spread apart a bit. *Hug it is!*

"It's good to see you—twice in one weekend!" I said as we settled into seats facing each other. *Just be relaxed.*

"I'm glad you could make the drive up." Her bright smile was a reminder that she only ever said what she meant.

"Well, thanks for inviting me. Notre Dame isn't too far." *Two hours on the nose from the student parking lot to my parents' driveway. Easy.*

"It was great to have you on the men's panel at the Shine Rally," she said.

"It was good to see so many kids there. Some of them looked so young, though! Did it take you back to those junior-high retreats we went on? Awkward, right?" I shook my head a little at the rise of those memories. *I was definitely awkward then.*

"Yeah, really. You missed out on my awkward junior-high days, though. I was already a freshman when we met at the Planned Famine, remember?" Amanda said with a gentle laugh I had always loved hearing.

"Ah yes, the ever-mature freshman. How could I forget?" I teased, handing her one of the menus on the table. *No sense wasting a visit from the waitress.* "Would you like some coffee? I'm on my third cup already."

"No coffee, thanks. But I'll probably order some protein since I'm planning to go running a little later," noted Amanda. *As if she needs to run. Urgh, running is the worst.*

I looked back up from rescanning the menu. "If you're not fully committed to running, I'll definitely suggest the cinnamon apple pancakes with whipped cream, of course. Delicious." Her scrunched forehead made it clear she was not convinced. So I offered, "This place has the best breakfast in town, in my opinion. Anything on the menu should be good, and it's on me."

She turned her attention back to the menu. So did I. *This is going well! We're just two adult friends, catching up on life and enjoying each other's company. She seems comfortable, like she always did when we were kids. She set out to accomplish a lot, and she's already done it!* Of course, I had come a long way too. My own path was still far from decided, though.

JOINING SEMINARY

West Michigan, on the interstate
March 26, 2006
Late afternoon

"So what do you think about your visit?" My dad asked from the driver's seat. My mom was riding shotgun beside him. I was behind them on the passenger side of the oversized SUV. It was a smooth ride with plenty of room to think.

We had already crossed back into Michigan and had an hour and a half left on our return from my first visit to Old College, the undergraduate seminary program at the University of Notre Dame.

Thanks to my parents, the possibility that any of us kids might be called by God to be a priest or a brother or a sister was always a viable option for me. It was the same shot I had at being a businessman or a teacher. *Dad owns a real estate company, so I know how to pursue that.* The path to becoming a teacher was equally easy to see. *If I was called to be a priest, however?* I had no idea how to figure that out. As it came time to pick a college, I decided to let that question alone for four years. That is, until Mr. Oleck, who worked with my dad, told me about Old College.

Old College, as I learned, was a residence house at the University of Notre Dame. They welcomed undergraduate men who were trying to figure out if God was calling them to the priesthood or religious life. At the time, that just about described me perfectly. I knew just enough to know that I needed assistance to figure out whether God was calling me. And it sounded like that's what this program was all about.

What would it hurt to check it out?

I decided to visit Old College for an extended weekend. I took the stay seriously. I ended the relationship with my girlfriend beforehand. To give the seminary an honest consideration, I knew I would need a clear mind and heart.

"What did you think, Matthew?" My dad asked again, this time a bit louder.

His too-even tone, after the eagerness he had displayed all weekend, betrayed his attempt at nonchalance. He was doing his best not to influence my opinion. *Thanks for trying, Dad, but I can see right through you.* Mom played it all a bit cooler. *I wonder what she thinks.*

"I liked it." *Way more than I thought I would.*

I had just spent Thursday to Sunday living with the current undergrads in the program, waking up for 7:15 morning prayer, attending a few classes, going to daily Mass, eating, talking, laughing, and hanging out with the guys. After all of that, I found out it was everything I had heard and more. There was a serious commitment to being in the program. Joining didn't mean that you would for sure become a priest, but it did mean that you were serious about discerning God's will about it.

There was something about the seriousness with which the life was structured, combined with the joy of the guys in the program, that connected with me right away. *It's a lot like choosing to go on a retreat. You have to decide to be engaged, and whether to be serious about what you encounter.* I honestly did not expect to like it. *Looks like I was wrong again.*

"What did you like most, Eddie?" my mom asked.

"The basilica." My curt response left them to pick up the conversation between themselves. They too had been captivated by the main church on Notre Dame's campus. The Basilica of the Sacred Heart left an awe-filled impression on first-time visitors. I stayed quiet as I thought back on it.

My heart rose and swelled to fill the vaulted arches that extended high above, as my eyes darted greedily around the church. I stood still with feet rooted to the floor just inside the main entrance, struck immobile. *This is the most beautiful building I have ever been in!*

Four sets of narrow pews, divided by one main aisle and two side aisles, stretched forward with smooth curves and carved crosses. They certainly weren't built for comfort like the pale-green cushioned pews back at my parish in Rockford. These seemed to say, "Pay attention."

Stained glass reached high in double panels around the walls. Soft, colorful light filtered in on one side. Grand paintings of the Stations of the Cross set in detailed wooden frames hung offset from the window. The faces depicted in the crowd conveyed anguish or hatred or mockery. Central to each was Jesus, weighed down with accusation or rough wood, exhausted and in pain, yet still showing love.

My parents had already moved farther up a side aisle. The sound of their hushed voices played across the walls and over the mostly empty pews.

"This is what it feels like to be Catholic." The words rolled out without me forming them. The basilica carried the bass tones of those slipped words around the church. My parents turned together to look back at me. I knew I was grinning. *There'll be no hiding my excitement now.*

I willed my feet to walk around for a better look at the individual windows and paintings.

Large pillars, planted every ten feet or so, flowed upward into the ornate blue and gold ceiling. Paintings of saints and angels filled the deep blue, starry expanses.

Above the main altar, the golden, domed arches created a sharp distinction. Eight saints gazed down. The four evangelists were easy to pick out. *The other four aren't angels, too gruff. Harp and crown, that has got to be King David. Stone tablets, that's Moses. So that makes the others with scrolls two Old Testament prophets.*

I caught up to my parents near the sanctuary. Two short transepts extended at right angles and the main body of the church continued past the sanctuary. It formed a cross.

I peeled my eyes off the ceiling long enough to study the glittering tabernacle that towered upward behind the altar. The magnificent, golden structure made it clear that it held the most important thing on earth, the very Body of Christ. Humble bread, transformed into the Real Presence of Jesus, enclosed by a small metal door in vibrant blue. Golden pillars and spires rose up like a castle or an ancient walled city. Angels sang from the towers and the Lamb of Sacrifice stood atop, victorious.

"Yeah, definitely the basilica," I said quietly as I watched the trees and telephone poles whip by.

Mom and Dad had turned the conversation to the overall feeling of being on campus.

Everything was beautiful. The large open grass quads, rows of trees, statues galore, the old, stately yellow-brick buildings. Notre Dame didn't have the raw beauty of a forest. Yet it took the glory of God's creation and, like a manicured park, made it accessible and pristine. *It was glorious.*

The Old College program itself included tons of structured community prayer. *Adoration every day?* I had never gone to adoration for more than three days straight, and then it was often months before I went again. From what I had seen so far of the guys in the program, I was excited to live like them. *There's something different about them. They have a playful focus. Or is it a joyful seriousness? Or maybe a freedom born of structure? I can't quite place it. But I like it.*

No dating, they had said, though. The thought stung. I wanted to date. I wanted to get married. I wanted to have kids and raise a family.

"I always wanted to go to Notre Dame," I heard my dad say from the front seat. "Remember all those years ago, when we wrote the list of our hearts' desires, Patty? I jotted down, 'Attend Notre Dame,' but I never thought I'd get closer than going to a football game every other year. We got a tour of the entire place! I got to stay on campus! In the building Rudy was filmed in!" His voice resonated with childlike wonder. *This is awesome.* I caught the side of Mom's steady smile. Her eyes were joyful too. She had a peaceful, if not thoughtful, air.

Something's happening. Something beautiful.

AS SEEN ON TV

Notre Dame, Indiana
January 17, 2007
After dark

Urgh, I don't want to write this paper. I sat in my dorm at Old College, staring at my computer screen. Two semesters into seminary and already writing papers had lost its luster. *But I need to.* I had enjoyed my classes so far. On a good day, I could honestly admit that I liked learning. But even on the best of days, I did not like homework.

After staring at a Word document with only my name and the course title on it, I decided to check my email.

There was one new email. It was from Amanda. The subject read: LIVE TV, tomorrow night. Amanda and I had not been in contact for a while. There were so many new things that demanded my attention. It was difficult to spare time to focus on things that weren't right in front of me.

> *Hey friends and family!*
>
> *I'm writing to share an exciting update! Tomorrow (Thursday), I'll be a guest on EWTN's LIVE call-in show, Life on the Rock. EWTN's Global Catholic Network reaches over 250 million television households in 140 countries. It would mean a lot if you're able to tune in at 8 P.M. Eastern Time! Either way, please say a prayer that I will sing my best and speak confidently about the faith.*
>
> *Gratefully,*
> *Amanda Vernon*

I tuned in early to catch the show. After telling the other

guys in the house about Amanda, explaining how we knew each other from our youth groups, and stating that she would be on live tonight, I was able to control the remote to the TV in the common lounge of the seminary.

It took a bit of searching, since none of us knew the channel off the top of our heads, but still we tuned in before the show began. "Fase, why is this so important again?" Tim, my roommate and best friend in Old College asked. He looked a bit irked.

A terrible theme song started playing as painfully outdated graphics appeared. Two priests in their brown Franciscan habits were shown sitting on screen. *Not a promising start.* The other guys gave side glances. So far, they too were less than impressed. After introducing the night's show, the cohosts kept talking. *When is Amanda going to be on?*

At the first commercial break, when an advertisement for an easy-to-read study of Pope Benedict XVI's recent encyclical came on, followed by DVDs with talks about sexual purity for teens, some of the other guys started to lose their patience.

"How much longer do we have to watch this? Can we change the channel?" Tim voiced what the other guys seemed to be thinking.

"Hey, come on! My friend is on TV. I'm not going to miss it. Plus, she's really good. It will be worth it."

Just then, the talk-show set returned and the two Franciscans invited her on. Her hair was super long, straightened and shiny, with a bit of a curl at the ends. She was wearing a metallic gold and silver top, with sparkly black sleeves. Long gold earrings flashed in her dark hair.

"Fase, you know her?" one of the other seminarians asked, incredulity dripping off the question.

"Yeah, since middle school."

"You mean, you know of her," Tim clarified.

"No, I mean we are friends. We went on a bunch of retreats together." *And talked and laughed a lot.*

"She's pretty," came the obvious statement from another.

"Yeah, I know." *She's awesome.*

"Amanda, before we talk about your ministry of music, would you address the tragedy that happened this week? The community of Virginia Tech, and our entire nation, is mourning the senseless act of violence that took the lives of so many bright young college students."

What a way to begin. Amanda paused for a moment. Then she took a deep breath and said, "I'm not sure there are any words to take away the pain we're feeling this week. In the face of so much sadness, sometimes," her eyes brimmed with tears, "the best comfort is simply to stand by each other in the middle of the storm."

"That's beautiful, and very true," one of the priests said. "If you have a song that might offer some consolation tonight, we'd love for you to play something for our viewers." The guys were all quiet as the next shot showed Amanda behind the keyboard. Though her hair was different, she stood as I remembered her: behind a piano, exuding confidence.

She started to sing. A few more impressed looks were shot my way.

> It's a difficult time, for you my friend
> I watch as you cry, unsure what lies ahead
> My heart breaks to see the trouble you're in
> And for your sake my own tears begin
> As they wet my face and roll onto my hands
> Don't know why it's the case, and I don't understand
> What good could come from this for you
> But I know that from above, God cries too

By the end of the song, her voice rang out strong and powerful. When she finished the moving piece, she joined the friars to continue the interview. She gracefully transitioned from her emotional reflection on shared suffering, to cheerfully speaking about her music and her faith.

She took a few live calls from people around the world. Amanda answered eloquently and boldly. I found myself leaning forward, grinning and nodding along to her replies. *I wish I could ask her a question.*

"Where can people learn more about your music ministry, Amanda?" the host asked. She responded, "The best way for people to follow my progress is through my website!" A banner with the web address popped up across the bottom of the screen. The hosts gave their thanks and goodbyes, and the credits rolled.

"That was a lot better than I thought it would be!" Tim offered as he scooped up the remote and changed the channel.

You'll Find Him

Verse 1

Not a day goes by
That I don't think of him
I remember his voice
And I wonder how he's been

Pre-Chorus

I'm not asking
If he's thinking of me too
It's enough to know
I'm loved by You

Chorus

I don't have words
To thank You for this gift
I don't have songs
To express just what it means
When I lay my head
On my pillow each night
Lord, search my heart
And there You'll find him

Verse 2

Seasons change
Some things remain
Years go by
He's still on my mind

Bridge

Bring that boy a better joy
Than I could be for him
And I will be content
Knowing You are holding him
He is Yours but You are mine
And all You have You give me
My heart's at peace tonight

TOUCHDOWN JESUS
AMANDA

Anna's House
Sunday, March 15, 2009
9:17 A.M.

The menu met the edge of the table. "Definitely the veggie omelette," I said.

"Great choice," Matt confirmed as he set his menu on top of mine. "It's been fun to see your progress from a distance. I was trying to remember, besides the rally yesterday, when's the last time we saw each other in person?"

"It was a year and a half ago, for the football game." *Yet another day with Matt that I'll never forget.* Before Matt could respond, the waitress returned. My smile couldn't be contained any longer as I recalled the events leading up to that blessed reunion.

AN EXTRA TICKET AND A BOY NAMED EDUARDO

Grand Rapids, Michigan
October 4, 2007
Dusk

By the beginning of Matt's second year in seminary, my career was taking off. After the live interview on EWTN, I had been invited as a guest on various radio talk shows and interviewed in Catholic newspapers. My dad helped me to officially incorporate as a music company (I called it Joyful Noise), and I hired a youth minister with excellent people skills to field calls and emails on my behalf.

While finding a specific niche and growing from there was a time-tested business model, this was about more than a financial enterprise. On the one hand, I was a natural entrepreneur. On the other, my heart's desire was to share the beauty of my faith through music. Between playing music part-time at St. Francis, writing new music, and giving concerts across the nation, the dream of using my musical gifts to tell people about Jesus had come true.

After a summer of travels, my friend Cecilia invited me to catch up at her downtown apartment in Grand Rapids. Cecilia was like an adopted big sister. Our conversations always consisted of soul-searching questions and laughter.

We sat on her back balcony with her sister Rose and our friend Domonique, drinking in the crisp autumn night around a candlelit table. The other girls, also a few years older than I, sipped wine. I had just turned twenty.

"Doesn't there always seem to be an Alejandro?" Rose asked over her wine glass. Her provocative question called to mind someone, *also named Alejandro,* who had been texting, calling, and asking me out on dates that summer. *Sorry, Alejandro. I'm skeptical about men, and I'm in love with a seminarian. It's complicated!*

"There usually is," agreed Domonique. We leaned in, anticipating a good story.

"There totally is! Or Eduardo," chimed Cecilia. Our laughter danced across the rooftops of the Heritage Hill neighborhood.

After swapping stories of men named Alejandro and Eduardo, and reliving our favorite summertime escapades, Domonique left to get ready for work the next day. As Cecilia walked her to the door, Rose said, "Oh, Amanda. Cecilia's coworker offered us an extra ticket to a Notre Dame football game for this weekend. We're driving down with our sister Angelica this Saturday. Would you want to come with us?"

I caught my breath abruptly. Trying not to reveal my excitement, I said coolly, "You know how much I love football. Remember the two rules at my parents' house? 'You have to be Catholic, and . . .'"

Cecilia's voice sounded from the hallway, "You have to be a Packer fan!" she said, finishing my sentence as she reentered the kitchen. "We remember! We came over to watch a game that one time, and you made us wear Cheeseheads."

"Right, right!" I thought of the photo we took together, adorned in green and gold and cheese. *Notre Dame this weekend? Would Matt be there?* Consulting with my heart, the invisible force of foreboding was nowhere to be found.

"So what do you say?" asked Rose.

"Definitely!" I nodded happily. Then casually, I added, "Also, there is this one seminarian."

"There usually is," agreed Rose.

"And his name is Alejandro," I countered.

"No!" Rose and Cecilia died with giggles.

As their laughter subsided, I admitted, "Not really. But his middle name is Eduardo. Technically, Edward. But the rule still applies." We laughed until our sides hurt.

Back at home that night, I emailed Matt about our plans to visit campus. His response came through almost instantly.

Amanda,

It's great you'll be coming to Notre Dame next weekend! Yes, I'll be on campus then. If you'd like, after the game,

you and your friends could come over to the seminary for
a meal.

Just so you know, I caught your EWTN interview last
semester. My heart swelled with pride to see you answering
their questions so boldly. You're doing incredible things!
It'll be very good to see you again.

Feel free to text me when you arrive, and I'll meet you
wherever you'd like.

Best,
Matt

He was watching, after all! He's proud of me. He's excited to
see me!

GAME DAY

Notre Dame, Indiana
October 13, 2007
Morning, noon, and night

There's so much Matt will never know about that day.

He would remember how festive the University of Notre
Dame was. It was probably like any other game day on campus.
But it was my first time.

My first time . . .
    at Notre Dame.
    watching college football.
    seeing him, since we were teens.

He'll never know how the adrenaline rushed through my body
like electricity.

Sure, energy was high on campus. Streams of students sauntered past in blue, gold, and some green. Preemptive cheering and prerehearsed chants sounded throughout the parking lot and between school buildings. The anticipation coursing through my veins, however, was because of him.

My friends and I were tailgating at the open hatch of their SUV. "Hey, Amanda, is your friend meeting us soon?" Rose asked, a hot dog in her hand and sunglasses on her face.

"I'll check to see whether he texted!" Searching for my phone in my bronze bag, I looked down at my dark jeans, bronze Skechers, and Notre Dame hoodie. It was my first purchase of sports gear without a Green Bay Packer logo. I had been overjoyed to pay the cashier, though, because it was for him.

He'll never know how difficult it was to breathe when he appeared across the parking lot.

Long, casual stride.

Hands tucked into his jean pockets.

The year's student t-shirt across his broad shoulders.

I'm sure he would remember Touchdown Jesus beaming from the towering library behind us. A triumphant Savior with arms uplifted in victory.

He'll never know how much I loved hearing his voice.

It was even deeper than in high school. "Hey," he said. And I knew.

It wasn't just me.

It wasn't all in my head.

I could tell—he felt it too.

He'd remember talking with Rose, Cecilia, Angelica, and me. In between laughter and hot dogs and root beer, he might even have caught their side glances at me. They held that delighted expression, as if to say, "He's so great."

He asked me to tell him about leaving college. Up until that day, it was the hardest decision I had ever made. And there he was, glowing with pride. It was like he understood the reasons and he believed in me.

He probably wouldn't believe how many times he said, "It's not a sure thing that I'll become a priest. It's only discernment at this point." He wasn't trying to send me a hidden message, though. He was just being honest.

Maybe he'd recall pulling that well-worn rectangular card from his wallet. "Look what I still have!"

He handed it to me, so eagerly. Why? Not because he was pleased with himself, but because he was proud of *me*, 'cause he knew how hard it was to live what we professed, and he wanted to show me that I wasn't alone.

> Believing that my sexuality is a gift from God, I make a commitment to God, myself, my family, and friends, to use the gift of my body and sexuality to bring honor, respect, and dignity to both God and myself. I choose to live a chaste life both now and in the future vocation to which God calls me.
>
> Signed: Matt Fase
> Date: 6/22/03

The fear that tempted me in high school shattered, the nagging questions: *I wonder what Matt's doing this weekend? I wonder who he's with?* I always tried to push those doubts aside, but they had persisted. Until that moment.

I returned the card, tempering my emotions.

"Yeah, those retreats were so great," he said. "They definitely helped me get here." He looked around with both humility and gratitude. And then it was time to head into the game.

Before we went to our separate seats inside the stadium, Cecilia stopped us. "Time to document, guys!" She motioned for us to look toward her camera. Angelica made faces as we posed for the photo.

He stood close to me.

His hand against my upper back.

His shoulder lightly pressed against mine.

"Great! One more!" said Cecilia, examining the image on her phone.

The cool breeze caressed our faces, the autumn sun smiled down. He wasn't trying to get something from me as he lingered. He just didn't want to leave.

We met Matt for dinner at the seminary after the game. We sat around one of the large, rectangular tables under the fluorescent lights in the dining hall. He regaled us with tales of morning prayer, quirky professors, and fellow seminarians. He listened raptly as my friends talked, and talked, and talked. We all laughed so hard.

He'll never know how much I noticed.

I noticed . . .

> his happiness.
> how comfortable he was.
> how he had no idea how much I cared for him.

"Would you like to see anything else on campus before you go?" Matt asked as we stacked our plates and trays.

"Yeah! We need to stop at the bookstore," Rose said.

"Amanda hasn't seen the Grotto yet," reminded Cecilia.

"Very good! We'll swing by there first, and then over to the bookstore?" he offered hospitably.

> Massive rock, carved out in the middle
> Vibrant, green vines clinging tightly to its exterior
> Wrought-iron stands displaying hundreds of lighted candles
> The darkness without, illuminated by the light within

The Virgin, in white and blue
Hands folded in supplication
Head bowed, humbly, as if listening to a small child
She watched us, from her own hollow in the
     beautiful grotto

Rose and I knelt on one of the low, wooden beams designed for that purpose. Cecilia and Angelica went inside the glowing cavern to light a candle. Others knelt nearby or stood to watch from a distance. Hushed conversations mingled with murmured prayers. Matt stood, several feet behind me. I closed my eyes.

"Dear Lord, if Matt comes to kneel beside me," I prayed, "I'm going to tell him the whole truth tonight."

How . . .
     I wanted so fiercely to be with him.
     I'd never been so drawn to any other man.
     I became a better woman by being near him.

Hail Mary, full of grace, the Lord is with you, I recited, in my heart. Matt didn't move.

Blessed are you among women, and blessed is the fruit for your womb, Jesus. Still the empty space beside me remained.

Holy Mary, Mother of God, pray for us sinners, now and at the hour of our death. He wasn't coming.

Amen.

Then, a tap on my shoulder!

"Ready to go?" Rose asked. I nodded. The knot of grief in my throat expanded. We walked side by side, Matt and I. He conversed with my friends along the way, graciously, genuinely.

"We're heading inside, Amanda," Cecilia said with a kind, knowing smile. We had arrived at the bookstore. My friends each hugged Matt, as if they'd known him forever. As the doors closed behind them, he and I were alone in the entryway. The cathedral ceilings towered above, and my heart throbbed within.

"This has been great seeing you, Amanda."

"It's been great seeing you too, Matt."

An invisible force urged me to say goodbye. So I said, "Okay, I'd better join my friends. Thanks again for hosting us."

"You're very welcome." Matt's voice soothed my ears and eased some of the tension in the back of my neck. He stepped closer and pulled me into an enormous embrace. An equally immense sigh escaped my lips. I allowed myself to relax in his arms for a few moments.

When I finally let go, Matt smiled down at me before walking out of the entry doors.

He'll never know how grateful I felt, driving away from campus that night.

Cecilia navigated toward Michigan. In the backseat, the warm Notre Dame sweatshirt wrapped me like a comfortable blanket, or like Our Lady's mantle of blue and white. The night air didn't account for the chills running up my spine. I couldn't recall a happier day.

It was all my favorite things: laughter, football, prayer, friends....

And then, there was Matt.

Driving away from the University of Notre Dame, the gentle sense of caution that had accompanied thoughts of Matt for years penetrated my heart, reaching between joints and marrow.

> Not a swift disjunction
> Not a sharpened ax falling
> Rather, the separating of softened clay

In the hands of a potter
Pulling, stretching, and finally
Ripping apart

A deep, aching pain, emanating from my chest
Traced up the back of my neck
And then down to my toes
Pressure, tearing me in two
Settling like an anchor against my sternum

A severing

More agonizing
Than I ever would have expected
And yet producing the surprising impression
Of open space
In an instant, I could inhale more deeply
Though each breath threatened another round

For years, I longed for Matt to really know me. Yet, I'll never tell him what happened to me in that Notre Dame hoodie and those bronze Skechers. He broke my heart, in the best way possible. And because I want what's best for him . . .

He'll never know.

TOUCHDOWN JESUS
MATT

Anna's House
Sunday, March 15, 2009
9:17 A.M.

Amanda folded up the menu and set it back on the table in front of her. "It's been fun to see your progress from a distance," I continued as I set my own menu down. "I was trying to remember, besides the rally yesterday, when's the last time we saw each other in person?"

"It was a year and a half ago, for the football game," she reminded me, smiling more deeply this time. As the waitress returned to take our orders, I smiled too, into my coffee. *That was a good weekend.*

GAME DAY

Notre Dame, Indiana
October 13, 2007
Daybreak

"Blessed be God," Fr. Kevin, the formation director of Old College, began the divine praises.

"Blessed be His Holy Name," the twenty of us Old Colle-gians added our voices to the prayer. We knelt at the wooden pews of the seminary chapel.

"Blessed be Jesus Christ, true God and true man." *Thank you, Lord, for this holy hour today. Morning prayer, Mass, ado-ration. What a powerful way to start the day!*

"Blessed be the name of Jesus." The hour spent before the ex-posed Body of Jesus in the Eucharist was mostly quiet aside from the Rosary we prayed together, a song, and prayer at the opening and closing. Still I couldn't help but think of prior moments spent in prayer. Surrounded by my peers singing out, praising God with pure intent, those moments in my memory were always led by her.

"Blessed be his Most Sacred Heart." *Amanda. I'm going to get to see her again today!* After following much of her progress through her thorough and frequent website updates, I felt like we were still so close. I, of course, did not have a website. *I'm sure she doesn't think of me much.*

"Blessed be His Most Precious Blood." *Be with her, Lord, in her life and ministry. Help her to lead others to You.*

"Blessed be Jesus in the Most Holy Sacrament of the Altar." Shouts from a raucous group of visitors penetrated the walls of the old Log Chapel. That kind of distraction was common on a football weekend. The old wood and steel door thumped and rattled as someone outside tested the lock.

"Blessed be the Holy Spirit, the Paraclete." The sign reading "Private prayer in progress. Please do not disturb" was clearly not enough for the curiosity of some.

"Blessed be the Mother of God, Mary Most Holy." We un-dergraduate seminarians and our formators savored these last moments of peace before our God, before we dove headfirst into the fray of game day at Notre Dame.

"Blessed be her holy and Immaculate Conception." *Amanda must already be on her way down!* A touch of nervousness rose as I thought of talking to her again and of the prospect of meeting her three friends. History had proven that her friends were awesome and very bold. *If Amanda likes them, then I'm sure I will too.*

"Blessed be her Glorious Assumption." *I'm in the seminary now.*

"Blessed be the name of Mary, Virgin and Mother." *The priesthood is the path I'm discerning, for now.*

"Blessed be St. Joseph, her most chaste spouse." *I'll be glad to share a day with Amanda and her friends.*

"Blessed be God in His angels and in His saints."

As we finished the prayer, Fr. Kevin blessed us and placed the luna in the tabernacle. Though Jesus was no longer present to our eyes in the form of that consecrated host, I knew that He was still present among us. *Lead me along your path.*

THE GROTTO AND THE GOODBYE

October 13th, 2007
After dark

The University of Notre Dame campus was settling down after the game-day festivities. The visitors were heading home, and students were shuffling, head down, toward their dorms. *Much more calm than the morning.*

Somehow, I had even more joy in my heart than when the day began. It was surreal. *How could I be this happy on a day the Irish lost?* It hadn't been much different than any other game day—prayer, tailgate, football, and food. It was a simple formula. Yet the skip in my step told me that today was different. *I suppose it may have something to do with my guests for the day.*

I took a long look over at Amanda as the five of us walked to the final stop before they left. She was quiet, as though she were still kneeling at the Grotto bathed in the flickering candlelight. Her friends, on the other hand, were chatting away. The excitement of the day was still bubbling around them.

"It was great meeting your coworkers at the tailgate, Cecilia. That worked out so well. And we're glad you found us too, Matt!" said Rose.

"My pleasure!" I smiled back. "We always have a tailgate with the seminarians, but I was happy to get to do both." As I had anticipated, her friends were definitely very bold and absolutely unforgettable. They had been easy to pick out in the rows of tailgating Irish fans.

My chest swelled, and my feet stepped even lighter. I had been hanging out with four witty, beautiful women all day. Not only were they constantly laughing and smiling, it was often because of what I said. That was not what the typical day for me consisted of as a seminarian. Today was a welcome highlight to the start of my second year in Old College.

"Notre Dame lost, though!" bemoaned Angelica, the youngest and quietest of the three sisters. "Isn't anyone sad about that?"

"Oh, Ang. It's Notre Dame! Of course, we want our boys to win! But the main thing is the history and the tradition here, it just doesn't get any better—win or lose! Plus, it was such a gorgeous day," said Cecilia.

I scanned the sky, the trees, and the buildings. *It had been a gorgeous day indeed.* My eyes settled again on Amanda. She continued walking beside me in silence. A wide smile I neither could have nor wanted to stop spread across my face. She was so confident, so collected. Besides being happy to be around her, I didn't know what to think. She made me nervous and at ease all at the same time. My heart soared and my stomach knotted. *Man, women are confusing.*

I knew I liked making her laugh. And I knew I liked looking at her. *I suppose she isn't all confusing.*

She's doing ministry for real now. While I enjoyed reading her blog, talking with her about it was even more exciting. The joy and difficulty, fear and trust she felt toward her music shone forth as she told me all about it from her own lips. And I finally got the opportunity to tell her how proud I was of what she was doing. There was no doubt all of her great work came from a place of great love. She was clearly in love with Jesus. It was Jesus whom she followed. It was Jesus for whom she sang. She even left a prestigious university to set out on her path right away. *Amazing.*

"Thanks again for having us for dinner, Matt," said Rose.

Dinner. The thought rose up as I barked out a laugh. The looks from my fellow seminarians had been a telling indication that my dinner guests were both welcome and out of the ordinary. "I was happy to host. We always have great food after the game, and we always have plenty." Amanda's thoughtful gaze cracked a little smile. *Keep it rolling.* "How did everyone enjoy the Grotto?" I asked.

"Awesome!" piped Angie.

Rose sighed. "It's so beautiful."

"Oh yeah." Cecilia furthered their praises. "Anyone who visits ND absolutely must stop by the Grotto."

Amanda just nodded solemnly. *She's so bold and fiery on stage. In conversation she holds her own ground. She takes jokes well and usually fires back with one of her own. But what's this other part of her that's deeply reflective and mysterious? If it weren't for those occasional smiles, I might think she was mad about the day.*

A dozen questions rose up as possible ways to decode that mystery. But each seemed too weak or frivolous to draw any worthy response from those depths. The now-familiar desire to really know her focused my eyes on her as I smiled.

"Is this it?" Angie asked, pointing to the building ahead and to our right.

Rose picked up her pace and chirped, "Yep! We'd better hurry because they're closing soon."

As the three sisters reached the doors, I reminded them I needed to get back. They each hugged me goodbye, as if we had all been friends for years. Amanda and I followed the girls into the entrance. She stopped and looked up at me as they continued into the bookstore.

The doors closed behind Amanda's friends. It was just us now, standing close together between the two sets of glass doors of the entrance breezeway. It was a space that was tight, yet open. Those beautifully complex green eyes looked up at me. Everything else went out of focus. The grandeur of the atrium, the worries of not being enough, the rules and expectations I had agreed to, all of it paled in comparison to the beauty in front of me. The depths of mystery in those green eyes beckoned me in. I felt myself leaning in, being pulled closer to this woman who had brought me so much joy. I wanted, needed, to be a part of that joy always.

"This has been great seeing you, Amanda." I said, meaning every bit of it.

"It's been great seeing you too, Matt," she replied, not breaking her gaze.

The words brought a few thoughts back into focus. I wanted to say something, do something to express that desire to stay with her. *But how? And now we're here, about to go our separate ways. Even if I wanted something more from this, why would she? And where would that leave me? Embarrassed by some rejected grand gesture. Or worse, it would lead me headfirst to a place I know I am too weak to turn from.* My thoughts continued to spiral inward. I looked away.

"Okay, I'd better join my friends," she said, confirming my better judgment. "Thanks again for hosting us."

"You're very welcome," I said, shaking off the thoughts of what could be.

As I had with the three sisters, I reached out for a hug before I started off. She stepped in close. There wasn't a trace of awkwardness. Our arms wrapped around each other effortlessly. The top of her head came up to just above my collarbone. Touching my chin to the top of her thick head of curls, I drew in a breath. *She smells amazing. Was it flowers, or some kind of tropical fruit?*

I drew my breath in deeper to hold on to her sweet scent. Within the overlapping of our arms, I could feel my chest expand into hers. Amanda's atmosphere of aloofness dissolved. She pulled in tighter, molding to me. I felt closer to her than I ever thought possible. Her smell, her touch, her gentleness, her complete attention. In that moment, I held it all. With a gentle sigh, her shoulders loosened. She rested her head against my chest. *It feels so natural to hold her.* I soaked in the moment.

Then she stepped back slowly. I exhaled, and the world snapped into place again. A small group walked past on the path outside the glass doors. *That was probably too big a hug from a seminarian. I don't want to give the wrong impression. But man, it was so awesome to see her. Her friends were great, funny, and welcoming. I don't know if I've ever laughed so much before.* Not knowing when we would see each other again, I was thankful for the day.

It was pure joy. My heart filled my chest as I took in another deep breath. It was brimming over with happiness, contentment, excitement, and half a dozen other feelings bubbling together. A smile played around my lips as I spun around and walked away from her to head back to my community.

WITHOUT HER

October 13, 2007
After midnight

I stretched my legs out, down the entire length of the extra-long, twin-size bunk bed of my dorm room. Between walking back and forth across campus multiple times and spending the whole game on my feet cheering, they were pretty sore. But it was my cheek muscles that protested the most from their near constant use in aiding my laughing and smiling. Campus was quieted by the dampening effects of the loss, and most of the guys in the house were already in their rooms for the night. With the unseasonable warmth and the lack of airflow in the old building, I threw off my blanket. I was tired, but not quite ready for sleep.

Scenes replayed in my mind from a movie we seminarians had watched together. It was a romantic comedy about two unlikely best friends: a priest and a rabbi, and the girl they both fell in love with when they were kids. When she moved away to another state in junior high, the two friends began their journeys as leaders in their respective religious communities. The movie humorously depicted the reunion of the three friends as adults, and chronicled the ensuing love triangle as they navigated those same emotions from middle school.

One scene toward the end of the movie was of particular significance in our formation. As the young priest grapples with his strong feelings for the girl he has cared about for so long, he turns to an older, wiser priest for guidance. The older priest offers words of consolation: "If you are a priest or if you marry a woman it's the same challenge. You cannot make a real commitment unless you accept that it's a choice that you keep making again and again and again."

In our ensuing conversations about the movie, Fr. Kevin encouraged us to remember that discerning our vocation was both about God calling us, and about our response. If God was calling us to marriage, it would be to a lifelong commitment with one specific woman. And just like vows in a religious community, faithfulness would depend on our response to God's grace, rather than on passing emotions.

It was one thing to think about a hypothetical future without a wife or children of my own. Imagining that same future without one specific woman was more difficult.

From the bunk below, Tim asked, "Is it okay if I turn the light off, Fase?"

"Yeah, go ahead."

Could I live without Amanda?
>I haven't spent much time with her in the last couple of years and I've gotten by. I could keep getting by.

What would it be like to not see her smile?
>I'd miss that, I suppose. It's a very nice smile.

What would it be like to not hear her laugh?
>That I would miss. I'd be less joyful.
>But I do suppose there has been plenty of joy in my life. If the Lord's asking me not to hear that, He'd provide joy elsewhere.

What would it be like to not ever hold her?
>That's not a fun one to think about.
>The muscles in the corner of my jaw tightened, like I was eating a lemon.
>I certainly did want to hold her.

What would it be like for her not to be the one . . .
>I tell everything to?
>who knows me better than anyone else?
>who I'm able to tell about my bad days and my good days, about my small victories and little defeats?

I would miss her laugh and her optimistic approach to the little follies. I would miss her encouragement, her constant faith.

I closed my eyes, praying as I drifted off to sleep.

I suppose that's altogether not a very fun prospect of something not to have.

If You want something else for me, that's gonna be even better. If You're really calling me to this celibacy thing, it must be way better than I think. 'Cause without her laugh and her presence and her joy, what would I have?

I'd have You, my Lord. Only You.

Yeah.

That could be enough.

I Went to Paris

Verse 1

Before I left we were just good friends
Bye, bye, boy I got a plane to catch
In the streets of Paris, when he was not around
Love like rain came pouring down

Chorus

I went to Paris
Got a brand new heart
Castles, fashion, escargot
Priceless works of art
But the treasure I brought home
Was a heart full of love
For the boy I left behind in America
The boy I left behind in America

Verse 2

My heart of stone was erased
A new spirit took its place
In the City of Romance
I was flying free
When something changed inside of me

Bridge

Did I have to go far away
To see what was in front of my eyes?
Would it be too late to love
The boy I left behind?

Final Ending

Would it be too late to love
The boy I left behind
In America?

WHAT I COULDN'T SAY THEN
AMANDA

Anna's House
Sunday, March 15, 2009
9:20 A.M.

After a few bites of his pancakes, Matt asked, "Tell me about this boy." *This boy?*

"You mean my fiancé, David?"

"Yeah, David."

I cupped the right side of my face with my right hand and smiled wistfully like a child watching a lighted candle in a darkened room. *Where to begin?*

David Shaheen.

The son of a Polish mother and a Middle Eastern father.

With my pinky and my thumb spread wide, I traced both sides of my jawline down to my chin.

Catholic roots, running back to Damascus.

Unfathomably sincere: curious, intense, driven, persistent.

My fingers tapped lightly against my lips.

Every time he walks into a room, people turn their heads to admire him. Penetrating eyes, olive skin, spiky black hair. The lean physique of a soccer player.

David Shaheen.

My Confirmation Crush.

Clasping one arm over the other, I glanced around the restaurant.

He's a singer now, like his mom. Pure tenor voice, perfect for harmonizing with mine. He plays the drums too, like his dad, and he's always beatboxing. He's earning his degree in marketing at a state university. On a full-ride scholarship that he never cares to talk about.

I rubbed my hands together gently and then intertwined my fingers loosely.

Did I mention his humility?

He's worked two or three jobs at a time through most of college.

I touched the tip of my nose against my folded hands. *At first, I didn't believe him. "Nobody is that nice," I thought.*

I was wrong.

Finally, with elbows resting against the table and hands gesticulating animatedly as though sharing a wonderful surprise, I said, "David is so wonderful. He's driven, faith-filled, gentle. He's really soft spoken."

Matt interjected, "Yeah, he seemed soft spoken at the rally yesterday. As in, you couldn't hear him." Matt was referring to a talk that David and I gave about our dating and engagement. Though he hadn't matched my gregariousness on stage, David's sincerity, I thought, outweighed his nervousness.

That edge in Matt's voice. I've never heard it before.

Matt shrugged and offered a meager half-smile as I looked evenly back at him.

"David and I joke that we don't recall when we first met, because we've known each other as long as we can remember.

David grew up at St. Francis too. In fact, he was at that first Steubenville conference you and I attended."

"Really? David was at Steubenville?"

"Yep. He hung out with Kevin, mostly. He was pretty shy, so you probably never talked to him. David and I always got along, but we didn't become close friends until he started college." I drifted off a bit.

David didn't really see me for who I was until last year. Something changed, though, in both of us.

"Congratulations," Matt offered another half-smile.

"What about becoming a sister?" he asked. "Did you ever look into that?"

Is that why his words are sharp like the top of a barbed-wire fence? Is it because he wants to make sure that this is my true calling?

"I stayed open to the idea. There was never much inspiration for it, though. I did go on a retreat at a convent recently, just to kind of double-check. Matt, look, the singing in the morning was *terrible*. There's no way I could live like that."

Matt let out a broad laugh. "Right! You should hear all of us guys in the sem at morning prayer. When we've just woken up, croaking out, 'Morning has broken!' It's like, 'somebody fix it!'"

That's more like it. Isn't discovering our life's calling supposed to be the most joyful thing?

After our first few bites of breakfast, Matt asked, "So what about traveling? Any favorite places now that you've been around the world and back?"

Yes, there have been so many amazing places. And you were there, in my heart, each step of the journey.

"Australia was amazing for World Youth Day. Of course, Europe was stunning too. But you know all about that. Did you spend an entire semester there?"

"Yes, I spent all of last semester in Belgium. What was your favorite European city?" he asked.

"It was all beautiful. Paris, though. Paris changed me completely." *There's a reason they call it the City of Romance. How could I explain coming home with a new heart?*

"It's awesome how a new environment can change your outlook, huh?" Matt asked, astutely.

"It really is." I took a deep breath. *If he's ever going to hear this, it needs to be now.* "Immediately after that trip to Europe, I realized this strong affection in my heart for David. Maybe it was there before, but I just couldn't feel it. As soon as I got back home, it was obvious."

Across the table, Matt seemed to consider my words.

"You had a lot to do with it," I said, hesitatingly.

Matt tilted his head a bit, remaining silent.

"I was never interested in anyone else since the summer before my sophomore year of high school because I had the biggest crush on you. And at first I wasn't in a rush to tell you because I felt like dating in high school was typically shallow, anyway. But then, you joined the seminary. And, well, I didn't want to be that girl, you know?"

Continuing to study me quietly, Matt's silence was the permission I needed to share my heart. The words spilled out like an autumn rainfall in Paris. At each turn of the story, the theme of the morning readings flowed like a gentle stream.

When I was all out of words, I took a deep breath and concluded, "I just wanted to thank you, Matt. I've wanted to tell you this for so long, but I waited. Mostly because the feelings were current, until . . . now." Matt looked thoughtfully out of the window. Outside, clouds blocked the rays of sunlight. Our half-eaten breakfasts were cool on our plates.

Chapter 8

WHAT I COULDN'T SAY THEN
MATT

Anna's House
Sunday, March 15, 2009
9:46 A.M.

"Paris changed me completely," Amanda said. Breakfast had arrived, and we had already exchanged some small talk about her engagement and her music tour. In spite of my mental preparation for this meeting, I felt surprisingly protective when she talked about David. It seemed safer to ask about traveling.

"It's awesome how a new environment can change your outlook, huh?" I asked, remembering my semester in Leuven, Belgium. That entire semester abroad was comprised of things I never would have planned to do. As a kid I preferred the familiar—like visiting rivers in northern Michigan—not trekking across the ocean or trying to communicate with strangers in an unknown language. Yet surprisingly, I loved it!

"It really is." Amanda set her fork down and looked more earnest than I remembered seeing her. "Immediately after that trip to Europe, I realized this strong affection in my heart for

David. Maybe it was there before, but I just couldn't feel it. As soon as I got back home, it was obvious." *She seems genuinely convinced about him. I'm glad for her. Right?*

"You had a lot to do with it." *I had a lot to do with what?* I set my fork down too.

"I was never interested in anyone else since the summer before my sophomore year of high school because I had the biggest crush on you. And at first I wasn't in a rush to tell you because I felt like dating in high school was typically shallow, anyway. But then, you joined the seminary. And, well, I didn't want to be that girl, you know?"

Wait . . .

Wait.

What?

"I mentioned how I went to visit a convent recently?" Amanda asked. I nodded instinctually. "Well, my friend Christine went with me, and we studied this beautiful teaching by an Austrian professor called the *Philosophy of Friendship*. One of his college students asked how to differentiate between authentic friendship and infatuation."

*Wait, she had to discern friendship or infatuation **with me**?!*

"His advice was to spend time with the person you're thinking of," she explained. "Rather than imagining him to be a certain way, actually sit down across the table from him. As long as you can be levelheaded, of course," she added matter-of-factly. "That way, you see who the person really is and not just who you presume him to be. Basically, you build a real relationship, rather than a fantasy one."

Amanda . . . had the biggest crush . . . on me. What?!

"That advice on the retreat a few weeks ago stayed with me. Plus, I had already been asking God to show me what to do with all this. I talked to David about it too. We don't have secrets from each other. I told him how I felt about you for all those years. David agreed it would be a good idea for me to talk with you in person. So thank you, again, for meeting me."

My blank stare must have conveyed my mounting incredulity. She continued.

"Back in high school, the way you treated me was so inspiring. It was such a stark contrast to other guys I knew. So I decided not to date anyone else in high school. I mean," she clarified, "I would only have dated you. I didn't know what that would have looked like, though." She took a deep breath, then exhaled slowly.

Does this mean it hurt her to hear about Old College? Did I hurt her?

"It's kind of comical to think of now. You should've seen me when I found out you were going to seminary. I was devastated!" She said it with a laugh, but her words confirmed my fears.

"I stayed hopeful. I knew it was just discernment rather than a sure path to priesthood. I tried to start dating some other guys, though. That didn't go so well, for anyone. I was so bored. And they picked up on that unavailable vibe, even in college, you know?" she asked rhetorically.

She was thinking about me in college.

"Or, say, when I came down to visit," she referenced the football game again. "A couple of guys were trying to flirt with me in the stands. One of them asked for my number. When I said no, he said, 'Oh, it's 'cause you're only into white guys?' I laughed because, like, no! That's definitely not why. It was just one, specific white guy." Amanda laughed again.

She said no to other guys because of me? She thought I was more appealing than most other guys?

Shaking her head gently, she looked out of the window for a few moments. "Anyway. After that, I decided I wasn't going to date anyone else, unless you discerned out, or unless I could feel about someone else the way I felt about you."

Her eyes glinted mischievously when she turned her gaze back to me. With a lowered voice, she said, "You should've seen my mom. She was borderline distraught. Whenever she found out about different guys I had turned down, she was just like, 'What is the problem, Amanda?' How was I supposed to answer? 'I'm waiting for a seminarian. Sorry about that, Mom.'"

She was waiting for me? What else have I missed?

"So, you see, the trip to Europe was very important. The theme of the pilgrimage was 'A New Heart.'" Amanda closed her eyes for a few seconds, as if she were back in the streets of Paris.

She was still thinking of me in Paris? That was last semester!

Her green eyes opened again as she recalled, "I didn't tie it together until we got back home, but the Bible verse we used for that trip was from Ezekiel. It talked about all these things that ended up happening to me! *I'll pour clean water upon you. I'll take you away from your land, and bring you to a new land. I'll take your stony heart and give you a new heart.*" The Scripture rolled off her tongue as if it had been written just for her.

"The last day of the pilgrimage was in France. Nothing seemed different, at first. Then that night, a couple of the other travelers and I went running through the streets of Paris. We ran over the cobblestone streets, past these quaint cafes and delightful boutiques. Suddenly, I realized—I was so very happy. And somehow, I wasn't waiting for you anymore."

When she used to share her prayers and her dreams like this, she wasn't just throwing it out there. She was letting me into a place in her heart. And she wanted me to stay.

"As we ran, I pushed words out. 'I'm so happy!' The very next moment, the heavens opened! Warm, autumn rain descended like a waterfall over the city. It was incredible." Her eyes glistened. "When I came home, David was waiting for me," she said in a soft tone.

She wanted me to stay, but not anymore.

"David had already been trying to date me for a year!" More pep arose in her voice now. "I always turned it into a friend get-together. I'd respond with something like, 'Oh, this Wednesday, for coffee? Well, I'm hanging out with Ida then, so you could definitely join us.' He was so persistent, though. He would hang out in a group setting, and he had become such a great friend."

Oh, yeah, Ida. Wait, what about when Amanda played with my hair on the bus ride home from Steubenville?

"Now, I see that my feelings for you prepared me for David! Waiting for you helped me to focus on music, on building lasting friendships. It kept me from getting into harmful relationships. And then, when the time was right for David and me to discern our vocation, God changed my heart."

Is she choosing someone else because she thinks I'm going to be a priest? Nothing's set in stone yet!

Her confession seemed to be coming to a close. "I just want to thank you for who you've been in my life, Matt. Even if you didn't realize it, you made a huge difference." Her smile was gone but her expression still sparkled with joy nonetheless. "I've wanted to tell you this for so long, but I waited. Mostly because the feelings were current, until ... now."

Amanda dropped her glance down to the half-eaten omelette on her plate. Looking toward the gray snowbanks outside, I tried to rapidly process the enormity of what she had just disclosed.

She's saying it could have been me, all those years.

Yet, even though she wanted to be with me, she cared more about how God might be calling us. She's been praying for me this whole time. When we went up for that vocations call at Steubenville, she was serious about discerning God's will.

What about those retreats, when she sat next to me for every meal, or when we walked through the woods together? Or the time that kid asked if we were dating. She wanted me to say I was her boyfriend because she wanted me to *be* her boyfriend!

And that stupid red visor! When she wore it back at the bowling alley, it meant as much to her as it did to me. She didn't think the visor was cool. She thought *I* was cool.

It could have been me.

What have I been doing all this time?

Well, I've been praying for her. My petition has been as frequent as morning prayer.

> *Lord, bless Amanda. Keep her safe. Keep anyone from using her or harming her in any way. Bring into her life the right man. A man who will love and cherish her, a man who will lead her to You. A man who is better than me.*

She's saying that man could have been me.

Amanda's raw honesty begged an equally candid response. *She needs to know the whole truth! She's speaking so openly. I've got to tell her how I feel too.*

"Really? Because when I got your email about being engaged, I thought, *Man!* Because I always had the biggest crush on you too."

We sat on the plastic benches of Anna's House in silence. Amanda's eyes were contemplative, searching like the beams of a lighthouse, spanning across Lake Michigan. Her eyes traced a path from the window to our plates and back to me. Then I heard myself asking, "It's not too late, is it?"

Bad Timing

Verse 1

You don't know how many years
I prayed I would hear you say you cared
You don't know how many days
I held back, I gave you space
Now you're bold, now you're here
Well, I moved on
I dried my tears

Chorus

Next time show up sooner
Now there will be no next time for us
Next time speak up quicker
Now we will never be
Talk about bad, bad
Bad timing

Verse 2

You don't know how many times
I thought I could see love in your eyes
You don't know how many nights
I wished you could be there by my side
And now you say you felt the same
Well, I moved on when you went away

Bridge

This is the bridge
Where I'd like to fix this
Tie a bow, say it's gonna be beautiful
But you make me feel out of sync
I don't think I get your timing
Time brings change
And you are late

BAD TIMING
AMANDA

Anna's House
Sunday, March 15, 2009
10:07 A.M.

"There are no such things as coincidences." The phrase was a Dean Vernon favorite. Both he and my mom tried to bring the abstract concept of Divine Providence down to my real-life experiences. They taught their children that nothing happens outside of God's loving care, from the events that shape history to the intricacies of our daily lives. Furthermore, Jesus was inviting us into a childlike trust in our Heavenly Father to meet even our smallest needs.

According to our Catholic Faith, God is absolutely sovereign over every event. This isn't a far-removed, untouchable reality or a poetic platitude from long ago. Rather, the words of Jeremiah 29:11 are a promise meant for each and every person: "For I know the plans I have for you, says the Lord. They are plans for good and not for evil, to give you a future and a hope."

What makes Divine Providence even more mind-bending is the belief that God carries out his plan through the cooperation of His creatures. Consciously or unconsciously, each person is a part of God's good plan. And while He has a loving call for each and every one of us, he allows men and women to be intelligent and free, and to act on their own.

We can freely choose to cooperate with God's love, or to turn away from it. Either way, God (love!) is victorious. Even when we turn away from His love, choosing something foolish or even something blatantly evil, He's always ready to guide us back. Faith assures us that God only permits evil in order to bring good from it. Only in eternity will we be able to completely comprehend the nuances of His plan.

My grandma used to say, "God writes straight with crooked lines," to describe this same phenomenon. Even being taught all of that from childhood, it is still hard to see it in the moment. Divine Providence, in all God's goodness and greatness, is seen best in retrospect. In the midst of it, sometimes it's hard to see how on earth all of these things are part of that plan.

"It's not too late, is it?" A smile cracked to one side of Matt's face—in jest? His eyes squinted slightly, however, as though searching for signs of light against a misty horizon. Forgiving Matt's brash attempt at lightening the mood, I finally acquiesced by shaking my head good-naturedly.

"Well, I have four more years in the seminary. I don't know how many more months you have left," he gestured, one hand forward, pantomiming a serious question.

This time, he drew out a full laugh from my gut, one part shock and the other amusement. *Does he really want to make light of this entire conversation?*

He wasn't laughing along, though.

"Matt, no!" Reeling from the prospect of a flippant dismissal, I backpedaled. "You're joking, right?"

He just looked out of the window again, a hint of a smile returning around the left corner of his mouth.

"What were you saying about being in Australia?" he asked. *He wants to talk about World Youth Day? I must have really thrown him off.*

"Well . . . ." Description ensued. My mind was elsewhere as I spoke.

Matt looked into my eyes again, and this time his expression was penetratingly sincere. "You're good, though?"

He's not joking.

"Oh, Matt . . . yes. I'm good." His fingers hovered against the edge of the table in anticipation.

I always thought he cared about me but that he clearly didn't care enough to do anything about it. If he's telling the truth about his feelings, why the heck didn't he say anything all of those years? Was he not man enough? We sat in silence. Thoughts strained to form suitable words.

Bless the Lord.

In an attempt to calm both of us, I reiterated, "What I'm trying to say is that those years of waiting for you helped me arrive where I am today. God used you to bless my life."

"Oh! Well, I'm glad I could be a tool," Matt answered sarcastically.

"That's not what I mean. I'm so grateful for you. And I thought it was important to tell you." *Wasn't it important? Wasn't this worth saying?*

"I guess it just wasn't meant to be." Matt's small sentence, laced with regret, jolted me from self-doubt.

"No," I said, exasperation gathering. "We're free! We're free to choose whatever we want! Do I believe God is leading me to marry David? Yes. But I'm not marrying him because it's predestined." My pulse quickened with conviction. "I'm choosing David."

The weight of the moment hung thick in the air.

"And you're choosing to be a priest. If that's what you decide."

Matt shrugged in acknowledgment, if not agreement.

Bless the Lord.

How can I put this into perspective? An example surfaced from World Youth Day.

"So, I got to meet that priest I told you about—the one who teaches the *Philosophy of Friendship*—in Australia. He talked about how we each have this light of faith within us, like a small flashlight shining in the darkness. When we gather with others who believe in God's love, we bring our small lights together. At World Youth Day, so many beams united brilliantly."

Matt's mouth was still.

"That's how I feel about you and me! Yes, we had these feelings for each other for so long. And yes, it's confusing why we never realized how much we both liked each other." The ache that still resided deep in my chest tottered on the verge of reopening.

"We both, however, believe that God has been leading us." An invisible force was pulling, ripping into the edges of the scar tissue. "When you bring your light of faith, and I bring mine, and we put them together, maybe somehow we can see the good that God will bring from this." *Why does it hurt so much?* The fibers of my heart splintered anew.

Quietly, Matt asked once more. "So, no?"

Tears welled, forewarning an unwelcome bathing of my face. *For so many years, he's the only one I dreamed of. So many nights, I wished he could be there with me. So many times, I made decisions based on my feelings for him. Now that I've finally moved on, he confesses he always felt the same way. He's asking me to walk away from the life I've decided to live without him. And I'm saying . . .*

"No."

Anger.

Resentment.

Disgust.

Now he's asking? Now that I'm right in front of him. Now that he knows without a shadow of a doubt that I cared. Not back in high school, when he was surely dating other, more convenient girls. Not when I was waiting for him. Not when we still had time.

Outrage.

Disbelief.

Pride.

Searing, red-hot, as more questions churned. *Celibacy sounds like a good idea until someone really attractive is a legitimate option? It wasn't worth taking the risk back then. No! Not until I look easy.*

> *Bless the Lord.*
> > *Bless the Lord.*
> > > *Bless the Lord.*

Like a bubbling brook, the stream of Scripture trickled down, cooling the smoldering blaze of indignation.

> *Bless the Lord.*
> > *Bless the Lord.*
> > > *Bless the Lord.*

"We should pray," I said.

Chapter 9

BAD TIMING
MATT

Anna's House
Sunday, March 15, 2009
10:08 A.M.

Amanda smiled, tilting her head to one side. My mind raced on. "Well, I have four more years in the seminary. I don't know how many more months you have left." The possibilities of what the future held leapt out in front of me.

Amanda barked out a laugh, not a joy-filled melodic one. This was harsher, more surprised. *Where's that coming from?*

"Matt, no!" she said from behind a wrinkled frown. "You're joking, right?" Her tone implied very clearly that I had better be.

Joking?! She brought it up! Okay, slow down. Change the subject.

"What were you saying about being in Australia?" *She had enjoyed talking about that.*

"Well . . . ." She softened as she recounted more about her time singing and traveling for World Youth Day.

I tried to focus, but my thoughts raced around my head. An entire new set of possibilities blossomed. *She liked me the whole time! She didn't date other guys because of me! She was waiting for me.* All of the signs I had missed clarified before me. All of the old fantasies and thoughts and questions of what could have been chased everything else away. *I missed those opportunities at the time. I can't miss this one. I missed those because, even though I was always taken by her, I didn't say anything. I won't make that mistake again.*

But is that what she needs from me now? I want her to be happy. I need to know what's best for her.

I observed her earnestly as she continued on about World Youth Day. *So many layers!* There was the genuineness that she always had, excitement, pride, thankfulness, and a sense of accomplishment at what she had done. There was also the deep humility that rested on her faith and trust in Divine Providence. There was contentment as well. Yet there was also a sharp edge of sadness that mixed with reluctance. *Was that because of me?*

So I ventured, "You're good, though?"

"Oh, Matt . . . yes. I'm good," Amanda said with a sweet confidence that nearly touched on pity.

My fingers tapped lightly against the edge of the table as I continued to chew through the mound of thoughts piling up in my head.

New possibilities mixed with old memories, each new flash shoving the previous aside.

"What I'm trying to say is that those years of waiting for you helped me arrive where I am today. God used you to bless my life," Amanda said. She was trying to help me sort it out.

"Oh! Well, I'm glad I could be a tool," I said, calmly smirking at the irony. *I am glad to be used by God, no matter how He chooses to wield me. And I seriously missed a whole world of possibilities with her.* I hoped the self-deprecating joke might help soften the situation.

"That's not what I mean," came Amanda's defensive reply. "I'm just saying that I'm so grateful for you. And I thought it was important to tell you." Her tone was far more hurt than thankful. *Clearly, the joke was the wrong route. Now I'm making things worse. Bring it back. What will smooth this out?*

God's will be done. He's the reason we're even having this discussion, right?

"I guess it just wasn't meant to be," I offered.

"No," she fired back, even more irritated. "We're free! We're free to choose whatever we want! Do I believe God is leading me to marry David? Yes. But I'm not marrying him because it's predestined." Frustration and so much more seemed to be rising in her as she articulated each word. "I'm choosing David." Her statement hung in the air between us like an accusation.

The door to a world of new possibilities that Amanda had just opened with the confession of her feelings was closing swiftly.

"And you're choosing to be a priest. If that's what you decide," Amanda said, punctuating her choice.

Well of course it's our choice! It's not fate. And I haven't even decided yet.

"So, I got to meet that priest I told you about—the one who teaches the *Philosophy of Friendship*—in Australia. He talked about how we each have this light of faith within us, like a small flashlight shining in the darkness. When we gather with others who believe in God's love, we bring our small lights together. At World Youth Day, so many beams united brilliantly."

Yeah, that sounds beautiful. So why can't our lights shine together?

"That's how I feel about you and me!" Amanda continued with renewed excitement. *Okay, good sign.* "Yes, we had these feelings for each other for so long. And yes, it's confusing why we never realized how much we both liked each other."

But now we do . . .

"We both, however, believe that God has been leading us. When you bring your light of faith, and I bring mine, and we put them together, maybe somehow we can see the good that God will bring from this."

Like the good of us finally being together? Like the good of us expressing our mutual feelings and letting them grow? Like the good of us supporting one another for the rest of our lives as together we follow God's will?

Or am I missing all the signs again?

"So, no?" I asked, looking up at her from across the table with my head hanging down.

Tears welled up, illuminating her eyes like the emerald hue of a forest at dusk.

"No," she said with the finality of a closed book.

Only silence followed.

It could have been me. But it's not.

David is the man I've been praying for all these years.

> To keep her safe.
> To cherish her.
> To love her.

Amanda's voice shook as she suggested, "We should pray."

We began with the sign of the cross. I had no words.

After more silence, Amanda began.

"Dear Lord, thank You for allowing us to spend this time together today. We bless Your Name, and we thank You for bringing us into each other's lives." She paused, her voice breaking with emotion.

Yes, Lord. I am so very grateful for the gift Amanda has been, for all the joy, and song, and faith she's brought into my heart.

"We trust that something good has taken place between us, even though it seems so confusing right now," she continued, sniffling.

And I'm thankful to have played such an important role in her life, even though I had no idea at the time.

"We give all of this back to You, and ask You to use it for Your glory."

It's Yours, Lord, all of it is Yours.

The tenderness and trust that she put into those words settled over me. Tears streamed down her cheeks, curving then falling off her chin. *I want to comfort her, but I do not know how. I would give anything to ease her sadness.* Tears welled up in my eyes as my heart ached with hers. A few quick blinks and a sharp breath kept them from falling.

"Amen," I confirmed, crossing myself again. Amanda reached for a napkin to dry the tears that had covered her face.

Amen. Amanda's right. We need to remember where our friendship began. It was through God that we found joy together as kids, and through Him we continue to rejoice. Perhaps the meaningfulness Amanda shared with me today could help others as well.

I took a deep breath, sat upright, and squared my shoulders. True, the paths of possibility that spread out in that instant were dead ends. A few new possibilities remained, nonetheless, encouraged by her steadfast faith and clear zeal for ministry.

"Maybe we could give talks together some day," I posited, thinking of all the talks we had heard together.

"Maybe," Amanda said.

"So, the check, for the meal . . ." Amanda reached for her purse.

"Don't worry, I'll take care of it," I said, snatching it off the table. *That's at least one thing I can do right this morning.*

She stood up. "Thank you," she said.

I stood to say goodbye. I reached out to hug her. *How could we part any other way?* She stepped into the embrace and hugged back tightly.

"Goodbye, Matt," Amanda said, then turned and walked away.

I sat back down in the chair, check in hand. *I've never had a meal that opened up so many possibilities and then just as quickly slammed them shut.*

Grateful

Chorus

When I hear your name, I recall your face
Always with a joke around your mouth
It didn't work out the way I hoped
My heart broke
But look at me now
I'm livin' in love
I'm confident and I'm unafraid
And I'm grateful that you came

Verse 1

Not looking back, I don't have regrets
Not calculating what ifs and what coulda beens
It's just, knowing you makes me who I am today
Life doesn't always go the way I plan, my friend
Sometimes, it's better in the end

Verse 2

I always wanted the best for you
I wanted to see you spread your wings and fly
Didn't know it meant that I would have to go
Life doesn't always go the way I plan, my friend
Sometimes, it's better in the end

Bridge

How can a woman be strong, without a little heartache
How can a man get bold, without some loss along the way
The world's best lovers discover, heartache's not the end of the story

THE ONLY ANSWER
AMANDA

Grand Rapids, Southeast side
Sunday, March 15, 2009
Late morning

> Elbows thrusting backward
> Faster
>   Faster
>   Faster

> Heart pounding, vibrating in my throat

> Flexed legs propelling me
> Faster
>   Faster
>   Faster

> Questions
> Allegations
> Disappointments
> Loathing

> Of him
> Of men

Of myself
Of the way things are

What about beauty?
Slam
   Slam
      Slam

Rubber soles colliding with concrete

What about goodness?
Slam
   Slam
      Slam

Lungs stretching wide
Straining with tension
Stinging with cold

What about truth?
Laugh
   Listen
      Be open

All of it, a ploy?
To use
   Dominate
      Discard

Doubled over
I gasped for breath
Why? My voice shouted

After running two and a half miles from my parents' house, I halted at a busy intersection. The clamor of the traffic paralleled the chaos inside me. Heaving from the rapid pace of my run and the painful accusations of my heart, I finally listened for God's response.

No words came. Only a sense of silence, deeper than passing traffic and turbulent thoughts. And then, an image of a man appeared in my mind's eye. Black hair, dark eyes, a gentle smile. *David.*

All was well. And all was forgiven. I turned around and ran back home.

THE ONLY ANSWER
MATT

Rockford, Michigan
Sunday, March 15, 2009
Late morning

There were so many signs I missed. Did I ignore them? "I just didn't see them," I said out loud to my reflection in the bathroom mirror of my parents' house. I peered into my own eyes, searching my soul for answers.

All of my interactions with Amanda had always been so exciting, life-giving even.

My fingers tapped lightly on the countertop. *How did I miss it?* She would have been perfect for me. She always laughed at my jokes. She was bubbling with joy. She was stunningly beautiful. She lived her faith with passion. She trusted deeply in God. And she even liked me! For SEVEN YEARS! *If only I had known.*

Clearly, she had been waiting for me for so long. Yet she cared about what was best for me more than she cared about dating me. *Maybe that's why I missed it? Because she was keeping it hidden?* Yet thinking back on all our interactions, I could see now that she was always affectionate and warm. *No . . . she was showing me. I was just oblivious. What else have I missed?*

Lord, why didn't I see?
  You weren't ready, came the answer.

Well then, where were You?
  I've always been with you.

So where are you now? I raised my hand to my chest, pressing firmly on my heart.
  Right here. Always here.

All the laughter, prayers, songs, love that we experienced together flashed before me again. I couldn't help but smile in the face of so much joy.

Hold on to the good.

Breathing out a long, steady breath, I closed my eyes. *Might as well put my new discernment skills to work here.* We were both seeking to hear God's call. That in itself brought a sense of assurance that He allowed our lives to follow these specific paths.

Her commitment to Christ is captivating. It shines forth as she leads others to praise Him in song. And now, she will continue to serve God in a new way, as she enters into the vocation of marriage. Continue to guide her, Lord. Bless Amanda and David.

I opened my eyes and stared at my reflection. A peaceful face gazed back. My gray eyes still held the loss of what might have been. Yet shining brighter was the joy and relief of reconciling with God's will. *He knows far better than I! Not my will, but Yours be done.*

Your Secret

Verse 1

I know your secret
You tried to keep it
Your actions have been giving you away
Did you think I wouldn't notice
I'm not blind and you know it

Chorus

You love me
You might say
You've never even told me
It's more than you'll admit
But I know your secret

Verse 2

It's how you
Nudge me with your shoulder
When you're walking by my side
How you listen for days
As I overanalyze
It's how you
Always make me laugh
Even when I'm feeling blue
How you speak the words of comfort
When I don't know what to do

Bridge

You're secret's safe with me
I'll never make you feel weak
'Cause love is strong
It won't stay hidden
For too long

Chapter 11

NEW BEGINNINGS
AMANDA

Hayward, California
May 28, 2015
Early morning

THE BLUE HOUSE

Thick carpet in a dark, chocolate hue covered the living-room floor of our new house. Outside our large picture window, beyond the porch and garden, and across our small residential street, fog wafted over the distant foothills. Redwood forests, winding roads, and Spanish-tiled rooftops adorned the sloping green meadows.

My eye scanned up and down the street. *Our ride isn't here yet.*

I looked down at the car seat near the door. Mercedes, our eight-month-old infant, was already strapped in snugly, ready for our upcoming trip. Swirls of sandy-blond hair complemented her golden skin. *I'm so glad she's not crying.*

Hurriedly, I looked over the luggage gathered in a cluster by the door. *Diaper bag, two large suitcases, one pack-n-play, an umbrella stroller. I think we have everything.* Taking a deep breath, I tried to reassure myself. *It's all going to be fine.*

On the far wall, a brick hearth surrounded an artificial fire-place. Atop its white mantel were black wooden picture frames in various sizes. My eyes rested on the frame at the center, displaying white matte cardstock around a picture of David and me. Our smiles beamed from ear to ear in the image. On the cardstock were handwritten notes:

"May Jesus keep you close to His heart."

"I love you, Amanda and David."

"Happy forever!"

Reading the well-wishes of our closest friends and family members brought a bit more calm.

Another picture, to the left, showed a packed St. Francis Xavier Church on our wedding day. We had invited our entire faith community to attend the marriage ceremony. My eyes landed on a third frame. It was a silhouette of David and me on a hilltop in downtown Grand Rapids, against the twilight sky. A deep blue surrounded our outline. On the photo, in contrast to the darkened hill on which we stood, were words in a white font: "In the image of God he created them; male and female he created them.—Genesis 1:27."

Many people thought David and I were crazy for getting married so young. At twenty-one, we had tied the knot years before the average American. "What about saving more money? What about traveling? What about doing things for yourself?" inquisitive onlookers would ask. And that was even before the children started coming.

"What do you think about the Catholic Church's old-fashioned ideas about sex and babies?" It was another very personal question, but one that strangers felt comfortable asking upon learning only preliminary information about our lifestyle.

"I think the Catholic Church is more romantic than you could ever imagine," I would answer. Reactions ranged from polite laughter to outright guffaws. Usually that kept their attention long enough for me to explain the ethos of the Church's "no contraception" rule. "Every time a husband and wife come together in a marital embrace, they proclaim with their bodies, 'I love you freely, faithfully, and completely, and everything I have is yours! Even my fertility.'"

This answer typically drew raised eyebrows, conveying both shock and awe. Yes, it was a hard teaching. And yet, I found no one had argued with its beauty. Loving each other faithfully unto death, welcoming children as a gift from God and raising them in the faith—that's what we signed up for on our wedding day.

I looked down at my left hand. A goldsmith had converted the promise ring from my dad into a brand new piece of jewelry. First he saved the small diamonds to adorn David's wedding band, and then he melded the original gold and sapphires with my maternal grandmother's engagement ring. At the altar, when David placed it on my finger with the words *Amanda, take this ring as a sign of my love and fidelity, in the name of the Father, and of the Son, and of the Holy Spirit,*" I knew my promise had been worth the wait.

Breaking into my thoughts, little voices called out from the kitchen. "Where are you going, Mommy?" Jamal, our inquisitive four-year-old, led the charge. *Breakfast must be finished.* As the eldest, Jamal was persistent and pragmatic like his father, but his facial features were mine entirely. Chiara, our second born, burst into the living room after him.

"Yeah, Mommy! Where you going?" She flipped her wispy brown hair from side to side with all the spunk one might expect from a three-year-old diva. Before I could answer, Mercedes gave a soft cry. She raised her chubby hands and smiled back as I scooped up her car seat with one arm. Rocking her gently from side to side, I reminded Jamal and Chiara,

"Mommy's going on tour, with Mercede-baby. We'll be back in a few days!"

David walked in from the kitchen. He wore a red pullover and gray sweatpants with "GVSU," the initials of his alma mater, printed wide down one pant leg. David's jet-black hair was still spiked with styling paste from the day before. Unlike in our wedding photos from seven years earlier, rectangular glasses sat atop his chiseled cheekbones. A subtle shade of blue outlined the inside of the black frames, bringing out his thoughtful, deep-brown eyes.

"Hey, babe. Let me know when your ride's here. I can bring your luggage out for you," he said in his smooth, calm voice. I took a couple of shallow breaths. "You're going to do great!" David assured me, anticipating my need for encouragement.

I nodded gratefully.

Then a knock at the door got everyone's attention. A friend from church had arrived to drop Mercedes and me off at the airport. *Time to fly.*

IN THE GARDEN

Portland, Oregon
May 28, 2015
Evening

Feed her, change her, remember to turn on white noise so she can sleep . . . . Running through a mental to-do list was typical for a young mom. Traveling across the country on a music tour with an infant in tow was more rare. In the passenger seat, being driven through the bustling city of Portland, Oregon, I could see why—it was exceptionally stressful. On the other hand, it was incredible.

At twenty-seven, life had already surpassed most of my childhood dreams. The bulk of my professional life was spent

giving concerts at Catholic churches, plus writing and recording new songs. Right after Mercedes was born, we moved out
to California, where I could be an Artist-in-Residence at All
Saints Catholic Church. The part-time music ministry at the
parish afforded me the time to heal from childbirth without
sacrificing my music career as an independent recording artist.

There was no publishing company or record label paying
for my new projects, however. Instead, I turned to my tight-
knit community to finance, and eventually enjoy, my creative
works. Family, friends, and fans supported our new music videos and new albums. The creative discretion was mine, but I
made it all for them.

David was putting his business degree to work managing
my career. He scheduled tour stops, negotiated contracts, ran
our website and social media, and oversaw the logistics of recording projects. He even arranged for me to sing the National
Anthem for the Green Bay Packers! *What could be better, except maybe the Vatican?*

David also graciously cared for Jamal and Chiara whenever
I needed to travel away from home with Mercedes. Thankfully,
we planned tour stops around friends and fans who champi-
oned our lifestyle.

Friends like Matt.

As our tour guide and host for the weekend, Matt turned the
car away from a busy main road. He pulled over unexpected-
ly. "We're stopping here first." *Stopping where?* The sounds of
the neighborhood were vibrant. Highway noise mingled with
shrieks of joy from the public pool at the corner.

Lifting Mercedes out of her car seat, I draped a lightweight
blanket around her tiny body. She nuzzled her head under my
chin. In a different season of life, a spontaneous stop in a new
city would have been exciting. Yet, thrill was hard to come by
when everything felt encompassed in mist. My mind mirrored

the dense fog that often blanketed our new neighborhood near San Francisco.

I rubbed my face against Mercedes' smooth cheek. Postpartum depression was a painful cross in my life. *But she's worth it.*

Matt's excited expression was framed by a full beard. He was dressed in a floor-length, black robe, tied loosely at the waist with thick black cord. A black cape draped to his elbows and around his back. Small fabric buttons ran the length of the habit. A brass crucifix rested at his chest, tucked between two of the buttons. Around his neck was a black collar, finished off with a small, white, square piece of stiff fabric at the center.

We crossed the street. Then Matt lead the way up a short cement staircase, cut into the side of a grassy hill.

At the top, we found ourselves in a city park. The noise of the surrounding neighborhood was damped by pine trees, stretching tall, around a paved pathway. Down another cement staircase, larger than the one behind us, was a garden. At the center was a circular fountain, surrounded by row upon row of roses in every color imaginable.

"Oh, wow!" I said. My jaw dropped in amazement as I looked out over the rose beds.

"Nice, right? Would you care to take a closer look?" Matt moved toward the next staircase.

My heels weren't very tall, but they made the steps a little tricky while cradling Mercedes. "Hey Matt," I extended a hand.

"Certainly," he offered his arm to steady Mercedes and me as we stepped into a veritable prismatic wonderland.

We admired the flowers in silence for a few minutes. I thought back on how much had transpired over the six years since The Breakfast. Stopping to smell a yellow rose, Matt asked, "You said you really loved being at my ordination. If it's not conceited, may I ask what you liked so much about it?"

"Well, you weren't the only one ordained that day," I quipped.

Matt let out a huge laugh. "True!" he agreed. We continued our stroll.

I considered the question. Being at Notre Dame the month before to see Matt and his classmates receive the anointing of the priesthood was stunningly surreal. David and I decided it was important for our family to be there, even though only Mercedes and I were able to attend.

Yes, I need to tell him how much that meant.

"I thought I would be one of your friends there," I ventured. "But . . ."

"You were my *only* friend there," Matt laughed. He wasn't painting the whole picture. Around thirty parishioners from his parish in Portland had flown to the Midwest for the ordination. Not to mention many of Matt's family members and college classmates. But when it came to friends from childhood, he was telling the truth.

"What I realized was," I explained further, "I think we're close friends." Tilting his head down toward me, Matt froze in place momentarily, one leg out to take the next step. The moment held something new, and fresh, and beautiful.

Mercedes' chest was rising and falling gently against my breast now, as her eyelids blinked drowsily. The scent of her sweet breath mixed with the aroma of fresh pine needles and sweet floral notes of the garden.

"It's just amazing," I continued. "Because I always wanted to be close friends with you."

Matt relaxed his position, replying with a childlike grin, "I always wanted to be close friends with you too."

We fell back into pace with each other, walking through and around the garden. My internal fog was no match for Matt's contagious exuberance. Conversation flowed as smoothly as the bubbling fountain. We met Fr. John riding his bike through the park after a while. Matt's pastor and superior, Fr. John, showed palpable joviality.

"Hey, Matt! Hey, Amanda. How's the baby doing?" Fr. John inquired. Mercedes, switching between admiring her surroundings and cuddling into me, was the picture of contentment.

"She's great. How's the bike ride?" I asked.

"Oh, it's always wonderful! I'll see you back at the rectory. Enjoy this beautiful night!" He pedaled off, wearing a cheerful smile and a neon green helmet.

After several more laps, a young college student waved to get our attention. "Excuse me, but are you a Catholic priest?"

"Yes! I'm Fr. Matt." After introducing himself, and then introducing me, we invited her to attend my upcoming concert for young adults at St. Patrick Church in downtown Portland.

"I'll definitely come! I've been hoping to meet more Catholics here! Thank you so much." She seemed thankful to meet a priest not much older than she was.

Apart from these brief pauses that touched on our ministries, Matt and I reminisced over the not-so-normal course of our friendship in the past six years.

How David and I had invited Matt to attend our wedding. How Matt had been there as a seminarian to witness our union. How a number of years had passed without much thought of him. Basking in the radiance of married life, making a cozy bungalow into a home in Grand Rapids, and then quickly welcoming a son and then a daughter, my mind had been otherwise occupied. Until I started songwriting again.

How, even as new life and new love overflowed, it became clear that Matt hadn't ever left my heart. Once more, I had tried to finish the song "Move On." Instead, a fresh piece spilled out. Before heading to the recording studio, I shared the lyrics and an explanation over social media.

"Bad Timing"

This song comes from years of feeling unrequited affection toward someone, then firmly moving on, and only then learning he felt the same toward me all along.

Today, happily married to someone else, I am at peace about the way this went down. I could not have imagined a better outcome. However, those feelings of hurt and confusion and incredulousness are still fresh on my heart when I think back on the ordeal.

So this is me opening that wound and writing from that place of simple irony.

Would you like to hear the song in a studio recording? Consider backing my project by making a pledge, and please join me in praying for success in this campaign.

Shortly after sharing, a notification appeared. "Matt Fase liked your post." Not long after, Matt backed the recording project. Following the album release concert, it felt commonplace to sit at a restaurant with my mom, my sister, and my husband. It was extraordinary, however, to have Matt and his younger sister with us. David had asked me afterward, "It's hard not to like Matt, isn't it?"

We saw Matt every once in a while, in Michigan or Indiana. Eventually, we invited him to become Mercedes' godfather, and then hosted him at our new home in California for her baptism on Thanksgiving weekend. More recently, I had hugged Mercedes close, under the breathtaking domes of the basilica at Notre Dame, as Matt vowed to give his life in the service of the People of God, as a priest in the Congregation of Holy Cross.

Our conversation led us around the roses, until the neighborhood children's gleeful shouts subsided and the sun set. The bubbling of the fountain also ceased. All the while, Mercedes slept peacefully in my arms.

This is definitely not normal, but it's certainly mystifying. And maybe even exciting.

NEW BEGINNINGS
MATT

Portland, Oregon
May 28, 2015
Early morning

HOLY REDEEMER

Stepping through the breezeway into the sacristy (where priests prepare for Mass), I tapped my pocket to double-check for my keys. *It's too early to get locked out of the rectory.* A metallic jingle confirmed their presence. *Good, that is why I'm here anyway.*

I was dressed in my second favorite habit. Sturdy shoes, denim jeans, and a hooded sweatshirt provided the perfect barrier against the predawn chill of a new spring day in Portland. Around my neck, from a thin black cord, hung a silver cross and anchors, the symbol of my religious community.

I opened the door leading into the dark sanctuary of the church. Candlelight from the red sanctuary lamp and the votive candles danced on the marble. *Thank you, Lord, for this place! And for calling me to serve.*

Consecrated celibacy. Why would a man freely make such a choice? When lived with integrity, the vows of poverty, chastity, and obedience call into question our world's fascination with wealth, pleasure, and power. After only one year as a fully professed religious in the Congregation of Holy Cross (*Congregatio a Sancta Cruce* in Latin, or CSC for short), I had personally experienced how the vows were far more about what I stood to gain than about what I was giving up.

The day of my Final Vows, I stood with my five classmates in the Basilica of the Sacred Heart on the campus of Notre Dame, as we each stepped forward and said "forever." I grinned like an idiot through the entire Mass. Forever! *God loves me more than I could ever know, more than I could ever express.* My profession of Final Vows was my response to that love. *That was the happiest day of my life.*

I crossed to the light switches on the far side and flipped a few on. *Let there be light.*

At my Final Vows, I was joined to an indivisible brotherhood within our congregation. The Constitutions of Holy Cross outline our Rule of Life, Guiding Principles, and Spiritual Understanding. One of my favorite Constitutions states:

"*The footsteps of those men who called us to walk in their company left deep prints, as of men carrying heavy burdens. But they did not trudge; they strode. For they had the hope.*"

As a family of priests and brothers, we CSCs share all our possessions. The phrase "common purse" sums up the practical implications of our vow of poverty. It means that all our monetary resources are first pooled and then distributed as the community discerns, for our various needs and ministries.

Though the lights were on, I felt the solitude of the empty church. I crossed back down to the side door. I twisted the Allen wrench and pushed in the bar. *One unlocked, four to go.*

Meanwhile, taking the vow of chastity allowed me to give myself away completely to the People of God. In the absence of forming my own family with a wife and children, I essentially married the Church. With Christ as the ultimate Spouse of the People of God, my "yes" to the priesthood symbolized His total gift of self.

Lastly, the vow of obedience (to those in authority in Holy Cross, according to our Constitutions, and to the pope as well) unlocked a new freedom to serve willingly, wherever my superiors asked me to go. Obedience came with the assurance that God would be present wherever I'm called, to lead and to guide me. As I strode up the aisle toward the main entrance, gratitude for my vocation welled up inside my chest. *I've certainly seen Him leading in my first ministry assignment.*

My first assignment was this Catholic parish and elementary school, Holy Redeemer, nestled in the heart of the Pacific Northwest. From the delightful variety of restaurants and microbreweries to the rugged, untamed wilderness of snow-capped volcanoes, rushing waterfalls, and mossy rain forests of towering trees, the entire region of the country was unlike any other. The people had welcomed me with open arms.

Their excitement about me isn't about me, though. I propped open three sets of white, wooden doors. *It's about who I represent.* Then I unlocked the large glass doors leading to the street.

At my final profession, I was ordained as a deacon to serve at the altar and preach the gospel. As of the last month, I was finally ordained a priest of Jesus Christ.

"In persona Christi" is a Latin phrase meaning "in the person of Christ." Those words summarize much of the Catholic tradition of the priesthood, passed on by the laying on of hands, beginning with Jesus and his apostles, all the way down to Pope Francis and every priest ordained as a minister of Christ.

I couldn't contain the joyfulness of my vocation. With each new day of the priesthood, God's glory shone brighter in my soul.

I looked down at my watch. *6:43 A.M. Oh, time for prayer!* As a local community, we prayed the Liturgy of the Hours before

Mass every morning, and I'd be celebrating the Mass today. *I still can't believe that's a thing I get to do.*

IN THE GARDEN

May 28, 2015
Evening

Dinner had been great. *Well, the food was delicious as always. The company was interesting, to say the least.* I drove the familiar route back from the weekly community night at the University of Portland. All of the Holy Cross religious in Portland were invited. Being there every week was an important way for the pastor, Fr. John, and me to stay connected to our wider religious community. I was the youngest of the priests and brothers gathered, with the average age being closer to sixty. We were a cast of characters seeking to follow the Lord together.

And so, I had made this drive back to the parish for eleven months' worth of Thursdays—as a seminarian, a deacon, and now, a priest. *This time is different, though.* Mercedes gave a gentle coo from the backseat. *This is definitely the first time I have driven back to the parish with an infant in the car.* Amanda looked back at her. *It's also the first time I've driven back to the parish with Amanda in the car!* A grin broke out on my face as I marveled at that fact. *I can't believe she came out to visit me! Well, she came out to perform in Portland, and we offered a free room. But still!*

There was still a lot of daylight left, even though dinner was already through. *The days are so long out here. No sense rushing back.* I turned three blocks early and parked on the side of the road.

"We're stopping here first," I told Amanda. *She hasn't had the opportunity to see much of Portland yet, and the Peninsula*

Park Rose Garden is a must. I hopped out of the car and went around to the passenger side to help her get Mercedes out. *She doesn't seem that excited. Well, that should change once she sees it.*

"All set?" I asked as Amanda wrapped Mercedes in a blanket. "This way." I nodded to the small rise of grass that ran along the road. I grabbed the black rope hanging down my side and gathered up a bit of the fabric of my cassock so I didn't step on it as I walked up the cement stairs.

At the top, I paused to look out over the park. *I still can't believe a place like this is only a few blocks from where I live! What a blessing!*

"Oh wow!" Amanda said as she finally made it up the short flight of steps. Her eyes lit up as she hungrily took in the beauty before us. She had been more subdued today than she had often been. *More thoughtful, perhaps?* But the fountain, roses, and manicured setting seemed to wake her up. I found myself smiling widely at her wonder.

"Nice, right? Would you care to take a closer look?" I offered. She nodded and I led the way down the brick steps leading straight into the center of the garden.

"Hey, Matt," Amanda said, still at the top of the stairs. She extended her arm. *Baby, heels, and she's jet-lagged. Of course I should help.* "Certainly," I offered my arm and we stepped down into the roses.

LOOKING OUT BACK

May 28, 2015
After dark

It feels good to sit down. I have no idea how many laps around the garden that was, but I'm sure it was more than I've ever taken before. It also feels good to have shorts on. The Holy Cross habit was an impressive visual display of the religious life, but it was also very warm. My flip-flops and t-shirt rounded out my summer evening attire. Amanda had also changed. Her snug pullover and loose athletic shorts belied the fact that she had just put a baby down to sleep. Although eight years had passed and three kids had arrived since she had visited me in college, she was as beautiful as ever. *Thank you, Lord, for the beauty with which You surround me.*

The sun had disappeared completely behind the hills to the west. Amanda and I now sat on folding chairs on the third-story back porch of the rectory. Mercedes' baby monitor sat keeping vigil just inside the door. *What an amazing evening! Mass and dinner with my community, an epic stroll through a rose garden, all the while sharing deeply with a good friend as we rejoice in our vocations. Thank You, Lord, for all of this!*

In the eleven months I had been stationed at Holy Redeemer, I finished most nights on this porch. Its height provided both a wide view, and relative privacy, since few people ever really look up. I often stood there surveying the church, school, parking lot, and playground. *Thank You for this place, Lord. It has brought with it challenges, that's to be sure. But above all it is a blessing. Thank You.*

We sat in silence. Enough words had already been said. The stillness of the summer evening settled on us. Over our shoulders and through the window, the sanctuary light burned next to the tabernacle of our chapel. On a night such as this, the wall didn't matter. The humble porch became the sanctuary of a grand basilica extending out over the neighborhoods.

Thank You for these people. Help me to serve them well. Help me to love your people as You love them.

Bless Amanda. Continue to give her the strength, courage, and faith to share her gifts with Your people. Thank You for allowing me to help her as I am able. Bless her family and her ministry.

I smiled, as the possibilities of how our ministries could one day combine danced through my head.

May Your will be done.

Providentially

Verse 1

I want to give you what you want
I want you to have it just the way you'd like to
I want you to feel it deep down in your soul
But I want you to be whole, even more

Chorus

Sometimes life is better than you hoped that it would be
Sometimes love is sweeter than you dreamed
When what you really wanted comes to be
Providentially

Verse 2

I want your soul to be
Light as a feather
Smoother than water
Innocent as a child
Like molten lava filling every vessel
The Good Lord pours you into

Bridge

You can take those wants
Try to deny them
Try to hide them
Try to grasp them for yourself
Or you can place them in the hands
Of someone who understands
How to make the sparks of your desire
Into a blazing fire

SANTA CRUZ
AMANDA

Santa Cruz, California
Saturday, January 30, 2016
Early afternoon

MAYBE WE'LL GIVE
TALKS TOGETHER SOMEDAY

In addition to being my employer and our place of residence, All Saints Parish was also our main community in California. Cristina, one of the members of my young adults' choir, "All Saints Unplugged," was in charge of the upcoming All Saints confirmation retreat. And so, that December, I had volunteered to help her by leading music for the upcoming retreat.

When Cristina needed another priest to help with Mass and adoration, my ears perked up. *I know just the person.* And then when she needed someone to give the "relationship talk," the wheels in my head really started turning.

I asked David what he thought about Matt flying in to celebrate the sacraments and to give a relationship talk with me on the retreat. David was keen on the idea, but suggested that Matt and I take one step at a time. "Let's see how this talk goes first before we assess anything for the future." Matt likewise agreed to the invitation on the condition that this would be a one-time deal.

So here we were, two months later, at a beautiful retreat center about an hour from Hayward. The grounds were comprised of dozens of cabins, nestled in the redwood forest of Santa Cruz, with a stunning wood and stone chapel at the center. The 150 high-school students had been listening raptly to the forty-five-minute presentation called "Where's God in Your Real-Life Relationships?"

After a whole day without their cell phones, they had settled into the peaceful ambiance of the retreat center. They listened, enthralled, as I told them my own story, with the theme of Jeremiah 29:11: "For I know the plans I have for you, says the Lord. They are plans for good and not for evil, to give you a future and a hope."

By their ardent expressions, my description of childhood hopes for an unbreakable romance seemed to resonate. We already covered how I had fallen for a kid in a red visor, how that hadn't worked out since he went away to college, and how my heart was ready for David at the right time.

A family picture appeared on the projector screen. David's handsome face, Jamal's broad smile, Chiara's evident spunk, and the bunches of golden ringlets around Mercedes' cherub cheeks drew an audible "awwww" from the teens. A few squeals of joy came from the girls in the front row.

"I can't say too much about David without crying, guys." On cue, tears welled in my eyes. *Happens every time.* "I love this man so much. So should we end here with 'They got married and lived happily ever after?' Which would be true! Or, do you want to know about the twist in the story?"

"Twist! Twist! Twist!" chanted boys in the back. Applause confirmed the general vote.

"What about the other guy?" I asked the audience. "The one I fell in love with when I was fifteen?" The teens nodded. "Well, after David and I got engaged, I was still thinking about him."

Audible gasps revealed their shock.

"Hear me out! I waited for this kid for *seven years*. I really wanted the best for him too! What do you think—I would just forget who he was because I loved my fiancé?"

Expressions of puzzlement peered back at me.

"David and I both agreed it would be good for me to seek some closure. So, I sat down with him one day, over breakfast, to tell him the story. And he said,"

The teens leaned in, on the edge of their seats.

"'I always felt the same way about you!'"

Frowns of disbelief crossed a number of their faces.

"And *then* he said, 'It's not too late, is it?' How do you think I felt in that moment?"

Groans were audible. "Terrible!" "Mad!"

"Let me sing about it, 'kay?"

Sitting at the eight-foot Steinway grand piano, I banged out "Bad Timing," with all the sass of an angsty teenage breakup song. Everyone was laughing along by the end.

With the final notes, I called out, "At the end of that conversation, I said, 'We need to pray!'" My look of desperation and sheer irony drew more laughter. "So we prayed, 'God use what has happened between us, as confusing as it is, for Your glory!' Afterward, he took a deep breath and said, 'Maybe we'll give talks together someday.'"

I let the statement hang out in the open air for a while, as I surveyed the chapel with a secretive grin. The atmosphere of the room changed. Some teens shot back a look of perplexity, while a handful of them were clearly having a lightbulb moment.

"I'd like to introduce you to someone," I offered matter-of-factly. Super-charged anticipation spread across the entire audience now. "Between the time of that breakfast and today, he became my best friend. In fact, he's the godfather of our youngest daughter." Murmurs broke out.

"You see, the college that he went away to was actually a seminary. You know, the place where a man studies to become a priest." Someone over to the left yelled, "No!"

"I'd like to introduce you to the man who unknowingly protected my heart for the vocation of marriage. He's now the happiest priest I know."

The girls in the front were squealing again. Across the room, heads turned side to side, searching for their surprise guest.

"Most people call him Father, but I usually just call him Matt."

Cheers, laughter, and clapping mingled together with the electricity usually reserved for a big-screen blockbuster.

"Please help me welcome…*Father…Matt…Fase!*" A standing ovation ensued as Matt made his way down the center aisle of the chapel.

I gave him a side hug and handed him the mic. "Take it away," I grinned.

After the students settled back down, Matt had a chance to explain his side of the story. He told what it was like to discern the priesthood. The students listened breathlessly as he shared his frequent prayer for me in the seminary:

> *Lord, bless Amanda. Keep her safe. Keep anyone from using her or harming her in any way. Bring into her life the right man. A man who will love and cherish her, a man who will lead her to You. A man who is better than me.*

Matt described the shock of finally hearing about my feelings, and the peace of framing the experience within the assurance of Divine Providence.

When Matt turned the mic back over to me, I sat down at the piano again to belt out one of my newest songs. This one had a distinctly more agreeable tone. Even so, it held the ache of failure. Unaccompanied, my voice rang out over the speakers.

> When I hear your name, I recall your face
> Always with a joke around your mouth

I sang on, about how it didn't work out, how my heart broke, but how I was grateful for it all in the end. I kicked in with the piano, upbeat gospel chords with jazz undertones.

> Look at me now
> I'm living in love, I'm confident, and I'm unafraid
> And I'm grateful that you came

A few students wiped tears from their faces. Mesmerized expressions filled the room. *Judging by this reaction to the story, Matt and I could probably share it again sometime. Would David be okay with that? Would Matt want to keep doing this, anyway?*

BLESS THE LORD

January 30, 2016
After dark

Late that night, following our talk, then free time and dinner, we all gathered under the tall wooden beams of the stone chapel again. My fingers hovered over the piano. Toward the front, Matt knelt in his cope—the long, open cloak reserved for only certain liturgical ceremonies. He was surrounded by the teens, who also knelt with folded hands or open palms.

Matt had been a hit with the students. The teens' admiration was obvious. "You're so brave!" they said. His ardent self-disclosure definitely demanded courage. *Matt isn't here seeking attention for himself. He's pointing us to Jesus.*

Up a few steps, on a simple wooden altar, was a large, golden monstrance. The white host within appeared to be illuminated. Behind the altar was a giant cross surrounded by huge glass windows. Outside, lights illuminated the redwoods. A golden glow spread up onto the towering branches.

I watched Matt's face for a minute. His eyes were closed as his lips sang along with the students, led by All Saints Unplugged and me. "No place I would rather be, than here in Your love, here in Your love." *A brother, a father, a confessor, a friend. He's so many things to so many people. But who am I to him?*

Since we began preparing for this retreat together, songs had poured out of me. It was an emotional moment, two nights before, when I played "Your Secret" for Matt. The two of us sat by the piano in the All Saints chapel. Jesus was also present in the tabernacle.

> You love me
> You might say you've
> Never even told me
> It's more than you'll admit
> But I know
> Your secret

With mist in his eyes, Matt conceded, "You're right. You're absolutely right." *Then why try to keep it hidden?*

If it's God's love, it doesn't need to be a secret. Yet, something—maybe embarrassment? Or was it shame?—seemed to lurk under the surface. *If it's anything other than selfless love, then I don't want it.*

If he wasn't physically attracted to me, maybe he could love without uneasiness. Temptation to curse my body—and a visceral hatred of the way men operate—hissed menacingly in my heart. *No. It's time to dwell on the good.*

I cued Unplugged to bring the music down, as I invited everyone into a time of silence. "If you start to become distracted, make those thoughts into a prayer," I said. "That distraction might be the very thing you need to work through tonight." Quiet settled over the chapel. A wave of queasiness passed through my midsection. My hand rested over my womb for a moment, where our fourth child was now several weeks along.

Over the microphone, I asked, "If you can recall one blessing in your life that you're grateful for, please raise your hand." Around the room, hands reached toward the tops of the trees outside.

David and I have four kids now! It was a thrilling reality. Having a big family of my own was a childhood dream coming true. The possibility of another round of postpartum depression, however, was terrifying. *At least I have this adoptive family for support.* I looked over at Unplugged. They were phenomenal singers, and even better friends.

Underneath the glowing redwoods, my piano notes sprinkled over the silence and began a new song. "Okay, keep your hand up there. If you can think of one more reason to be grateful, please raise your other hand." Throughout the chapel, hands stretched high.

I'm so grateful for All Saints Unplugged.

There was Lo, a college freshman, and former Hollister model. AC, who used to sing in a major-label pop vocal group until he left to find a greater purpose. Matthew, AC's younger cousin, who never greeted a friend without literally jumping for joy. Cristina, forever kind (and sarcastic), the violinist and director of the retreat. And Annalisa, our youngest member, resident queen of social media and more strikingly gorgeous than she knew.

AC shot me a warm smile. "Okay! Keep your hands up there!" I instructed everyone. "Now, let's make this song overflow with gratitude."

My friends began harmonizing passionately. "Bless the Lord, oh my soul! Worship His Holy Name." I loved Unplugged like my own brothers and sisters. I knew the feeling was mutual.

Fingertips to the piano keys, I pulled back from the microphone and listened to the voices crying out, "Sing like never before, oh my soul. I'll worship Your Holy Name."

The man draped in the garment of the priesthood had his eyes on Christ and his hands raised high. *I praise You for bringing us this far, Lord. There's no way this has ever been merely about physical attraction. Being drawn to each other as kids led us both to say "yes" to You, in the way that You were calling us.*

Do you want us to keep sharing this gift together, with Your people?

Open the door, and I'll walk through.

Chapter 12

SANTA CRUZ
MATT

Santa Cruz, CA
January 30, 2016
Early afternoon

MAYBE WE'LL GIVE
TALKS TOGETHER SOMEDAY

It wasn't butterflies flitting in my stomach. It was more like cornered bears getting ready to brawl.

Hearing Amanda speak to over a hundred students from Oakland, California, with the backdrop of a redwood forest would normally have been really fun. But this time, she was speaking unabashedly of falling in love with me when we were kids. *In love? Of course I've been in love with her since the day we met. But do I have to admit that? How could I ever say it out loud?*

"Twist, twist, twist!" the students cheered from all around me. *She certainly has them hooked.* In spite of the impending embarrassment, I grinned at Amanda. *She set this all up so perfectly. Relatable, engaging, funny, and infinitely applicable to their high-school lives. This talk is working.*

And we're doing this together. Even another wave of queasiness couldn't suppress the joy and the thrill of knowing that Amanda and I were really ministering together. *We're combining our gifts so well, that—*

"But there's still time, right?" Amanda quoted my words back to the high schoolers. The bluntness of the question combined with her dramatized expression of astonishment, shock, and anger produced groans and cheers aplenty.

My musing was cut short as a jolt of adrenaline surged. *Just about my time.* I sat at the back of the crowd on the center aisle. Some of the more astute listeners were starting to make the connection.

"I'd like to introduce . . . ." Heads whipped back and forth looking for the interloper. Adrenaline, embarrassment, anxiety, fear—they swirled like a firestorm in my blood. *I don't want to do this! I don't want to tell them! I don't want to share!*

But I do want to love them. Peace broke in and settled over the storm, tamping down the fear. *I trust, Lord.* The anxiety settled down. Excitement remained, and embarrassment. *Perfect fuel for the talk.*

"Please help me welcome . . . *Father . . . Matt . . . Fase!*" Cheers. Gasps. Shouts erupted as I slowly stood up.

Come, Holy Spirit.

BLESS THE LORD

January 30, 2016
After dark

"No place I would rather be, than here in Your love, here in Your love." Amanda sang the words that were bursting from my soul. *Here in Your love, my Lord. This place, resting in Your love, is perfect.*

I knelt looking up at the monstrance on the makeshift altar. Behind, a great bank of floor-to-ceiling windows looked out at the redwoods. All around and behind me the students joined their voices in prayer and praise. *We've gotten through to them. Probably not all of them.* But there they were with their voices lifted high in song, praying so tenderly. I closed my eyes and let the harmonies from her friends, *my new friends,* enwrap me in so much beauty.

"Set a fire down in my soul, that I can't contain and I can't control. I want more of You, God. I want more of You." The words sprang from my heart, lifted to God on the music. *You, Lord! You are all I want!*

"Let's take a few minutes to enter into silence." Amanda's voice said over the microphone. "If you start to become distracted, make those thoughts into a prayer. That distraction might be the very thing you need to work through tonight." At her invitation, a quiet settled over the chapel.

In the silence, I prayed one of the most powerful prayers I knew. I first heard it as a seminarian while on an eight-day silent retreat. It was a retreat that changed my life.

Lord of passionate love, stir the embers of my heart.

I pictured my heart as the remnants of a raging fire.

Lord of passionate love, stir the embers of my heart.

The gray ash cracked and broke off under the force of a mighty wind.

Lord of passionate love, stir the embers of my heart.

My heart glowed a bright orange and then burst into flame.

I thought back over the weekend so far, inviting the Lord to revisit the events with me. *Come, Holy Spirit.*

I recalled walking through the redwoods with Amanda after our talk. Nervous energy still bubbled out of me. *It's important for me to debrief. How do we think it went? What were the fruits?*

"Did you hear what Elizabeth told me?" Amanda inquired as we walked through the redwoods after our talk.

"I caught just the end of it. What did she say?"

"Just a second," Amanda said. She stopped strolling, closed her eyes, and placed her hands over her stomach. It was probably morning sickness. Amanda had told me the good news when she and her children picked me up from the airport that weekend. *Baby number four! What a beautiful gift for her and David!*

Something more than gratitude stirred within me. I watched her, eyes closed and new life blossoming inside. Haze started to play around the edges of my emotions. Giving this talk with her required that I be completely open, yet completely on guard. *Why does she make me feel so uneasy?* And yet, it was a happy unease. *What does that mean?*

"Okay, thanks," Amanda had said, looking around again. "Well, Elizabeth is about twenty years old. She said her boyfriend recently joined the seminary. It's been heart wrenching for her, to the point that she didn't want to volunteer today. She described asking God for some kind of answer, 'What should I do? I love him!' She arrived in time to hear our talk this afternoon. With so much gratitude, she told me, 'I'll never forget this day.'"

Thank you, Lord, for new life. Thank you for the work Amanda and I are able to accomplish together. I stared into the monstrance, resting in the silence. *There'll be just one more song before Benediction.* Meanwhile, a few lines from Amanda's new songs played through my memory.

My smile deepened and I shook my head lightly at the concept of being the subject of so much music. *I must be so vain to think these songs are about me.* While "Bad Timing" was cheeky, these more recent pieces were open and honest and penetrating. Sure, the name puns and inside jokes she folded in were funny, but that only pointed to the strength of our friendship. *What will her next song touch on? What will the next one reveal?*

"But I know your secret," Amanda's smooth voice sang gently in my mind. *She does. And I do.*

My confidence faltered a bit at the thought. *She's always floored me with her honesty and passion. This time it's directed right at me. And it scares the crap out of me.*

So what now? I grimaced. Old insecurities bubbled below the surface of my heart, threatening to erupt in fear, panic, and dread. *I'm not strong enough. I'm not strong enough to have her know how deeply I care about her. I'm too weak to know she thinks so much of me.*

Piano music began to play gently, signaling the start of a new song.

Amanda's voice brought us all back to the moment. "If you can think of one blessing in your life that you're grateful for, please raise your hand." Instantly, my hand raised high. *Thank you for this gift of the priesthood.* Countless moments bringing Christ to my people flashed in quick succession. The full force of the grace of my vocation settled on me, dispelling the emptiness of doubt and shame.

My heart is so full of love. Baptisms, weddings, hours in the confessional, prepping high-school students for confirmation—each was a graced moment of bringing Christ to His people. Anointings of the sick, ordinations of fellow priests, saying Mass .... *You didn't have to choose me, but you did, out of love, Lord.*

"Okay, keep your hand up there. If you can think of one more reason to be grateful, please raise your other hand."

I raised my right hand just as quickly. *Thank you for friends with whom your joy abounds.*

I'm grateful for Unplugged. From the moment I met that joyous knot of singers, we laughed. Getting stuck in the driveway was not met with panic but raucous laughter. The entire drive, every moment of downtime, and even time that wasn't free, was spent laughing. Mealtime had contained even more joy than food. AC, Matthew, Cristina, Lo, and Annalisa—we laughed so hard that we were doubled over and our sides hurt. *So much joy.*

We all sang with hands raised and hearts lifted.

> Bless the Lord, oh my soul
> Oh my soul, worship His Holy Name
> Sing like never before, oh my soul
> I'll worship Your Holy Name

The song's triumphant end was my cue. As presider, it was my role to lead the Benediction of the Blessed Sacrament. I gathered my vestments, stood up, and then stepped over to the back of the altar.

One of the teens, acting as an altar server, held the thurible—a metal incense burner, suspended from chains. I carefully spooned in a few heaps of the granular incense onto the red charcoal briquettes. Perfumed smoke arose immediately.

The server handed over the chains of the thurible. We were ready to begin the Benediction. I looked over at Amanda.

She was as I first saw her—at the piano, helping us pray. So much had transpired between then and now. Yet here we were, still seeking Jesus and finding Him through prayer. Not only that, but we were leading others in ministry together.

I've often said I don't get what I want. *Who cares what I want, anyway?* As Amanda watched me across the room, waiting for my lead, the happiness in my heart offered an answer: *God cares.* He cared about a seminarian who wanted to seek His will. He cared about a high schooler who wanted to be free. He cared about a fourteen-year-old boy who wanted to be near to her, and to be near to Jesus.

Filled with Amanda's joy—the joy of the Lord—I nodded, giving her the signal to continue. She and her friends, my new friends, began the "Tantum Ergo." I knelt in front of the altar.

> Down in adoration falling
> This great sacrament we hail
> Over ancient forms departing
> Newer rites of grace prevail
> Faith for all defects supplying
> Where the feeble senses fail

Billows of smoke rose upward. I breathed in, the sweet scent filling me. I held that breath, tasting that moment, that peace. I exhaled, surrounded by more joy and love than I ever thought possible. The song continued, as my heart cried out.

"To the everlasting Father and the Son who reigns on high." *You, Yourself, are all my delight, Lord.*

"With the Spirit blest proceeding forth from each eternally." *You have given me the desires of my heart.*

"Be salvation, honor, blessing." *This is Your call we answer. It's Your command we follow.*

"Might and endless majesty." *Love one another, as I have loved you.*

The music slowed. All eyes were on the Lord. And together we sang, "Amen."

EPILOGUE
AMANDA

San Francisco Bay Area
Monday, February 1, 2016
Early morning

From the lookout point just a mile from my home, rolling hills sloped down to meet the sparkling bay. Vibrant blue waves ebbed and flowed from the San Mateo Bridge to the south, to the Bay Bridge to the north, eventually meeting the Pacific Ocean underneath the fiery-orange arc of the Golden Gate Bridge. A magnificent treasure trove of Victorian homes, teaming highways, and soaring skyscrapers graced the San Francisco Peninsula, which stretched between the bay and ocean.

Matt and I stood side by side, taking in the view. The fog that often hung over the buildings and bridges had dissipated in the morning light. The city glistened.

"Isn't it beautiful?" I asked after a while. Matt looked toward me. He wore blue jeans and a hooded sweatshirt. His answer went without saying. Mocking his opaque sunglasses, I suggested, "You could take those off so I could see your eyes." He scrunched up his nose in response, but reached up to remove them nonetheless.

Matt blinked and then squinted toward San Francisco, complaining, "My eyes were made for the Midwest." I badgered again,

"Oh yeah, the sunshine must hurt a lot. That's gotta be hard." My blatant lack of sympathy was well received, judging by his chuckle.

"Did you get any nice letters on the retreat?" I asked.

At the All Saints confirmation retreat that weekend, the participants and leaders were invited to leave small notes for each other. Each of us had written our own name on the front of a brown paper bag, then stapled the bag to a giant corkboard in the foyer of the main gathering space. The bags acted as our personal mailboxes for the weekend. A supply of scrap paper, pens, and markers were left out on a table in the foyer. Whenever the inspiration struck, we could write a message of encouragement to leave in someone's mailbox.

Matt responded cheerfully, "I certainly did! And you?"

Sticking my hands into the pockets of my black track jacket, I felt the edges of one of the notes. "Me too," I said. "Especially this one poem."

A pink hue spread from Matt's cheeks to the tips of his ears. He pushed his sunglasses back on. "Yeah?" he asked sheepishly.

"Yeah, I loved it," I confirmed.

The night before, after All Saints Unplugged and Matt and I drove back to Hayward from the redwood forest, I read through the messages in my makeshift mailbox. There were loving memos from Unplugged, and inspiring letters from students. And then there was Matt's note. The folded segment of copy paper bore his handwriting:

> Amanda, Amanda
> I do love you so
> But of this you're aware
> For my heart you do know
>
> Such a blessing you've been

As I've journeyed along
Always there with a smile
And of course with a song

I know that at times
I'm distant or cold
Or lead with a joke
That's too hurtfully bold

I'm so deeply sorry
For the ~~hurt~~ pain that I've caused
So I want to say sorry
In the midst of this pause

Over

Quiet laughter leapt to my lips. I turned the poem over.

I know that some hastily
Bad written poem
Is far from enough
To fully atone

So I'll say one more thing
About you from my heart
I'm so thankful for you
And you do have my heart

— Godfather Fr. Matt
— or that awkward teen who oscillated between
confidence & fear, and who from the beginning was
enamored, impressed, & inspired by you. Which I
still am.

Happy tears blurred the page as I finished reading his poem that night.

Looking over the San Francisco Bay with Matt, a fusion of excitement and mystery surged. I was so grateful how the Lord had led us both and in awe that we were able to share the joy of it—not only with each other, but with the Body of Christ as well. It was too much to articulate or to contain. So I laughed instead.

After a few more minutes, we walked back down the hill.

As we approached my neighborhood, Matt resumed our conversation. "I'm kind of insecure about my handwriting. Plus, I rhymed 'heart' with 'heart,' in the poem. That's embarrassing. Plus—" Interrupting his apology, I assured him, "It was perfect."

With a grin and a shrug, Matt appeared to let his embarrassment go. He changed the topic and asked, "What do you think we could've done differently with the talk?"

Could've done differently? Why does he ask? What's done is done.

With a curious frown as my only answer, he rephrased the question. "It might be helpful to debrief. Say we were going to give this talk again. What would we change?"

Wait ... I thought this one was a one-time deal. I gave Matt an inquisitive look and narrowed my eyes. *He wants to keep doing ministry together?*

"I'm saying, I would give that talk again. Not every week. Or even every month. But, yes."

Really? This could be a thing we do regularly? Combine our ministries and help raise up another generation of Catholics together? Could we?! I mean . . . "Well, I'll talk with David," I said. *David will want whatever's best for our marriage and for our family.*

Matt and I had arrived at the Blue House. I was scheduled to play a concert soon, and Matt's return flight would depart that afternoon. Standing in the shade of our front porch, Matt removed his sunglasses. A tapping at the living-room window caught our attention. Chiara and Mercedes giggled and waved at us. Matt waved back before turning toward me to ask, "I guess that's our lot in life, right? Being watched." His eyes were searching.

"I guess it is. There are a lot of people watching us now," I said. Taking a deep breath, I recalled our prayer at The Breakfast. "Isn't that what we prayed for? That God would use this for His glory?" Gratitude beamed from Matt's face.

"That we did," he agreed. The feelings I had for Matt for so long reflected back at me through his eyes.

The reverence of a priest among his people.

The contentment of a compassionate friend in a rose garden.

The vulnerability of a hopeful heart, confessing tender feelings over breakfast.

The longing of a college student, embracing the one his heart desires, after a football game.

The excitement of a kid holding out his red visor to a girl who doubted whether any boy could really love her.

Where our youthful desires seemed to have died, something new had taken root. The dreams of our childhood had fallen like a tiny seed planted in the earth, only to grow up into a towering tree. The man he had become and the boy I once fell in love with were one and the same.

More pounding on the window.

"Well, I'd better get ready for my concert. You're okay staying here with David and the kids until they drop you off at the airport?"

"Definitely. I love your family," he said.

"We love you too, Matt."

A few hours later, behind the steering wheel of our minivan, I looked in the rearview mirror. Sunshine poured down on the little Blue House. Through our chain-link fence, I caught glimpses of my children, running merrily in the garden. My phone lit up with a text.

David: We'll take Fr. Matt to the airport this afternoon. He's watching the kids now while I catch up on work. Love you.

Heading out of our driveway, joyfulness reigned in my soul. Because sometimes, the best blessings come through the worst heartache. I laughed to myself as I turned out onto the main road. *Apparently, God's timing is the best, after all.*

P.S.
MATT

"... because of the abundance of the revelations ... a thorn in the flesh was given to me, an angel of Satan, to beat me, to keep me from being too elated. Three times I begged the Lord about this, that it might leave me, but he said to me, 'My grace is sufficient for you, for power is made perfect in weakness.' I will rather boast most gladly of my weaknesses, in order that the power of Christ may dwell with me. Therefore, I am content with weaknesses, insults, hardships, persecutions, and constraints, for the sake of Christ; for when I am weak, then I am strong."—2 Corinthians 12:7–10

Joy is Amanda's middle name.

Through my friendship with her, I have grown more than I ever imagined.

> I know myself in new ways.
> I understand new dimensions of God's love.
> I love more.
> I have more joy than I thought possible.
> I have healed from deep wounds in my heart.

The infected wound of pornography, which I mentioned in this book, stayed with me even into adulthood. The shame was crushing. Yet the painfulness of this struggle makes the blessing of finally overcoming it all the greater.

By God's grace, I have been healed.

To remain within the abundance of that healing, persistence in prayer and the sacraments is paramount. Likewise, the encouragement of close friends is invaluable. There are also a handful of men who hold me accountable to this healing. David is one of those men.

When I inquired after this "boy" all those many years ago, to try to find out what he meant to Amanda, I could not have fathomed all that he would eventually mean to me. He is an inspiring example of leading and living from a place of faith. He is a man who has built his house on the solid rock of God. The stability it provides can be seen in all he does, as a husband, a father, a businessman, and a friend.

One cannot love, truly love, Amanda without also falling in love with David. He has her heart. They are bound together as one flesh. To touch Amanda's heart is to touch David's. So I can say without hesitation, fear, or doubt that I love David.

I am eternally grateful for David's presence in my life. Without his help, we couldn't have written this book, nor would Amanda and I have the friendship that has resulted in so much joy.

First Edition Underwriters

This publication was made possible by
many generous backers, including:

The Andersen Family
The Bill & Shannon Brewster Family
John & Jodi Bunks
Scott & Debbie Fabel
Jaime & Chelsi Gerow
David & Renee Larsen
Alex & Katie Marshall
Dennis & Kim Moline
Marco Riolo
Mark Rogers
Dick Safranski
Mike & Tracey Shaheen

AMANDA VERNON is a recording artist of soulful pop music. This singer, pianist, and composer has shared her original music across the U.S. and in six foreign countries, at venues as diverse as World Youth Day in Sydney, Australia, and Madrid, Spain, to Lambeau Field for Monday Night Football. In 2018, she released Secretos Navideños, her eighth album. Originally from the Midwest, Amanda resides in Phoenix, Arizona, with her husband and their spunky collection of children.

Amanda's music and tour schedule are available at her website. You can also read her blog or request a concert for your next church or school function at **AMANDAVERNON.COM**.

MATT FASE, CSC, was born and raised in Rockford, Michigan. He attended the University of Notre Dame, graduating with a BA in Theology and Master of Divinity. He professed Perpetual Vows to the Congregation of Holy Cross in 2014. Since his priestly ordination in 2015, Fr. Matt has served as the Associate Pastor of Holy Redeemer Church in Portland, Oregon, and as the Campus Minister for Retreats and Athletic Chaplain of Stonehill College.

To invite Fr. Matt and Amanda Vernon to speak to your community, to see videos about *When God Wrecks Your Romance*, or to order the audiobook, visit **WHENGODWRECKSYOURROMANCE.COM**.

As a full-time independent recording artist, Amanda Vernon is completely fan supported. To help her share her music and feed her family at the same time, consider becoming an Amanda Vernon Patron. You'll receive exclusive updates about her artistic projects and early access to original content.

AMANDAVERNON.COM/PATRON